The Essential Guide Classroom Practice

The Essential Guide to Classroom Practice has been written with two questions in mind. These are the questions that are most important to all practitioners who seek to improve the quality of learning in their classrooms – what strategies work? And how do we implement them?

Covering all the areas that are key to effective teaching and learning, this text consists of over 200 practical strategies that secondary teachers can adopt and apply within their classroom. These strategies range from simple tools to improve the quality of questioning, to principles that can shape the whole approach to learning. Key topics covered include:

- The five-part lesson plan

- Developing thinking skills

- How to engage learners

- Encouraging collaborative learning

- Challenging and supporting

- Assessment and feedback.

A key feature of this book is the handy collection of 'top tens' that appear in each chapter, such as ten ways to use data in the classroom and ten ways to streamline your marking. The book clearly explains the benefit of each approach described and offers additional guidance on using websites and digital tools effectively in the classroom. Packed full of ideas, the book offers a one-stop shop for busy teachers.

Andrew Redfern is Assistant Head Teacher and Director of Sixth Form at Sheffield High School, UK, formerly with responsibility for teaching and learning. He is also a Specialist Leader in Education (SLE) and Senior Examiner for Edexcel.

The Essential Guide to Classroom Practice

200+ strategies for outstanding teaching and learning

Andrew Redfern

Routledge
Taylor & Francis Group

LONDON AND NEW YORK

First published 2015
by Routledge
2 Park Square, Milton Park, Abingdon, Oxon OX14 4RN

and by Routledge
711 Third Avenue, New York, NY 10017

Routledge is an imprint of the Taylor & Francis Group, an informa business

British Library Cataloguing in Publication Data
A catalogue record for this book is available from the British Library

Library of Congress Cataloging-in-Publication Data
Redfern, Andrew.
The essential guide to classroom practice: 200+ strategies for
outstanding teaching and learning/Andrew Redfern.
pages cm
1. Learning. 2. Teaching. 3. Effective teaching. I. Title.
LB1060.R385 2015
370.15'23—dc23
2014034733

ISBN: 978-1-138-80028-1 (hbk)
ISBN: 978-1-138-80029-8 (pbk)
ISBN: 978-1-315-75555-7 (ebk)

Typeset in Celeste and Optima
by Swales & Willis Ltd, Exeter, Devon, UK

Printed and bound in Great Britain by
TJ International Ltd, Padstow, Cornwall

For Ellie

Contents

List of figures   ix
List of tables   xi
Acknowledgements   xii

Introduction   1
   Who is this book for?   2
   The evidence base   3
   How to use this book   5
   Referencing system   7

1 A plan for learning   14
   The Five-Part Lesson Plan   15
   Planning in practice   23
   An answer to questioning   28
   Top ten ways to use data in the classroom   34
   Chapter summary   42

2 Developing thinking skills   44
   Creative thinking   46
   Reflective thinking   50
   Higher-order thinking   54
   Split-screen thinking   60
   Top ten graphic organisers for learning   68
   Chapter summary   72

3 Engaging learners   73
   Game theory   75
   Engaging with texts   87
   Active engagement   92

Contents

Making learning real 100
Top ten principles of effective classroom management 107
Chapter summary 110

4 Collaborative learning 112
Fostering shared ownership of learning 116
Encouraging effective participation in group work 121
Structures for learning together 125
Top ten digital tools for collaborative learning 136
Chapter summary 141

5 Challenge and support 143
Challenging students through extension activities 145
Personalised learning 152
Differentiation by choice 155
Questioning to stretch and challenge 163
Top ten strategies to support students 167
Chapter summary 172

6 Assessment for learning 173
Sharing learning expectations and modelling good practice 174
Questioning to review progress 179
Formative use of summative assessment 185
Self-assessment and peer-assessment 190
Effective feedback through marking 195
Top ten marking time savers 200
Chapter summary 202
Final words . . . 203

Bibliography 204
Index 206

Figures

0.1	Five Components of Outstanding Lessons	2
1.1	The Five-Part Lesson Plan	16
1.2	Sample lesson plan 1	22
1.3	Sample lesson plan 2	24
1.4	Sample lesson plan 3	26
1.5	Proportion of question types asked by teachers	29
1.6	Flight path, levelled	35
1.7	Flight path, predicted grade	36
1.8	Baseline sorting	37
1.9	Spiky profiles	38
1.10	Progress wall chart	40
1.11	Data analysis	42
2.1	The process of 'thinking about thinking'	45
2.2	The Creativity Wheel	49
2.3	Plenary Dice	50
2.4	Exit Signs	51
2.5	The Socratic Plenary	53
2.6	Picture Wall links	59
2.7	The Six Learning Junctions	62
2.8	The Conditions for Learning Model	65
2.9	Skills Icons	67
2.10	Top ten graphic organisers for learning	70
3.1	Where there is behaviour for learning, there are high levels of student engagement.	74
3.2	Example of a board game template	76
3.3	Diamond 9s	77
3.4	Materials Top Trumps cards	84
3.5	Cranium spinner	89
3.6	The Classroom Management Pyramid	110

4.1	The evidence-based research makes a strong case for the importance of learning together	113
4.2	Maslow in the classroom	113
4.3	Teaching spectrum	114
4.4	Six Learning Leader cards	118
4.5	Student Tutor card	126
4.6	System 1 table layout: the dinner party	130
4.7	System 2 table layout: inner and outer circles	130
4.8	Four-way Worksheet	131
4.9	Example from a Creativity Carousel	134
4.10	Digital tools for learning	139
5.1	The capacity for a teacher to challenge and support all students	144
5.2	Differentiation spectrum	144
5.3	Example of a QR code with audio	146
5.4	Example of a QR code with a geo-location address	146
5.5	Bloom's Challenge Wall	148
5.6	Accelerated Learning Contract	153
5.7	Lesson flow chart	158
5.8	Targeted Objectives	161
5.9	Question token	164
5.10	Solve It	165
5.11	Example of Questions that FLOW	168
5.12	'Hormone' Picture Clue	169
6.1	Evidence-based research acknowledges the importance of assessment for learning	174
6.2	USB visualiser and Talking Tin	177
6.3	Thinking Hats Writing Frames	179
6.4	Review Wheel	180
6.5	Trapezium Hinge Question	183
6.6	AfL Playing Cards	192
6.7	RAG Reflections	193
6.8	Peer Feedback Grid	194
6.9	Four-part marking framework	196
6.10	Medal and a Mission	199

Tables

2.1	A summary of the Creativity Wheel	49
3.1	Wildcard Quizzes: splitting the cards for different class sizes	81
5.1	Homework credit system	160
5.2	Summary of Questions that FLOW	167
5.3	Example of a Word Bank	169

Acknowledgements

I have been extremely lucky to work with many excellent practitioners in a range of schools since joining the teaching profession. In some way they have all contributed to this book and for that I doff my cap.

A special thank you to Keith Hirst and Kevin Stannard for their early support and guidance in writing this book and Dean Jones, Neil Plant and Matthew Turton for being a source of inspiration. For their valued contributions, I must also thank Louise Cline, Sean McGovern and Leander Jones, three outstanding teachers to whom I am indebted.

A big thank you to the team at Routledge for their encouragement and support, and especially Annamarie Kino for helping me make this book a reality.

A final point is that wherever I have borrowed from, adapted or modified the work of someone else, I have tried my best to reference it and acknowledge how it has shaped my own strategies, models and suggestions. If I have failed to do this fully, I apologise in advance and hope to be able to rectify this in future reprints.

Introduction

As the cover states, this book is a practical guide to teaching and learning. Many of the ideas and principles are applicable to education at all levels, but the main focus of this book is in secondary education. It has been written with two questions in mind. These are the questions that are most important to all practitioners who seek to improve the quality of learning in their classrooms: What strategies work? And how do we implement them? In order to answer these questions, each chapter draws on a range of evidence-based research to explore those issues that are paramount to successful learning. Issues such as differentiation, questioning, assessment for learning and collaboration are the subject of many a thread on the teaching and learning blogosphere and typically the focus of numerous in-school teacher training sessions, all because they are fundamental aspects of our profession. Within this book, you will find over 200 effective ideas to help teachers of any school or subject, or stage of their career, answer these questions and build their own strategies to facilitate outstanding lessons.

Since entering the teaching profession, I have spent considerable time reflecting on what makes an effective lesson, where all students are engaged and make good progress. I would wonder, and still do, why one lesson went well whilst another could just as easily be a bit of a flop. For some time I've played around with the notion of a formula for the perfect lesson; a set of principles that if applied correctly would lead to 'outstanding' lessons time after time. With my responsibility for teaching and learning at my current school and the CPD initiatives I am involved in, I have even more time to observe and reflect on this question and with some certainty I have come to the conclusion. . . there isn't one. Nevertheless, there are a number of characteristics that shine through and are common in any outstanding lesson – I will refer to these as the Five Components for Outstanding Lessons, shown in Figure 0.1. These five factors are facilitated through purposeful planning and lesson design.

In summary, effective learning takes place when students are actively engaged and challenged to work just beyond the boundary of their comfort

1

Challenge and support for all learners

Effective thinking skills

Assessment for learning

Effective planning and preparation

High levels of engagements

Collaboration between learners

Figure 0.1   Five Components of Outstanding Lessons

zone, whilst being given the right level of support to meet their needs. Students see learning as a social process; they collaborate and support one another, consequently taking responsibility for their own learning. They will use a range of thinking skills to acquire new knowledge and demonstrate the dispositions and behaviours for successful learning. Teachers will effectively facilitate learning and use assessment strategies to provide relevant and informative feedback, which students use to make progress towards their targets. Above all, teaching and learning is geared to ensure every pupil achieves their potential. This is the goal of every teacher and the principle on which this book has been written.

Who is this book for?

And now to my target market – the teachers for whom this book has been written – and how they might go about using it.

1.   *Teachers starting out* – if you are in this category, welcome. Teaching is a physically and emotionally challenging job, but it is just as equally

rewarding and worthwhile. As an ITT, NQT or RQT you will spend a fair amount of your time planning lessons, resources and schemes of learning. Chapter 1 has been written to help teachers do just that. The Five-Part Lesson Plan is a framework provided to help teachers design and facilitate effective lessons. The rest of the book then presents a smorgasbord of ideas that will slot nicely into this framework. Sir John Jones refers to the profession as the 'Magic Weaving Business' and I hope this book will equip you, as a new recruit, with a wide range of ideas to help you go 'weave' your own magic.

2. *Teaching and learning geeks* – by 'geek' I refer to those teachers who have a deep interest and enthusiasm for effective classroom practice – anything that helps teachers support the learning process. If you get excited by the latest educational initiative, follow an assortment of teaching and learning gurus on Twitter or spend a little too long developing resources than some would consider socially acceptable, then I am referring to you. But let's face it, we've all got a bit of teaching and learning geek in us somewhere and that can only be a good thing. If you are a teaching and learning geek, I hope this book will be a source of inspiration with strategies you want to try, adapt and develop into your own great ideas. Now, go forth and geek out in your own lessons!

3. *Leading teachers* – implementing effective teaching and learning in your own classroom is one thing, but when you are required to develop it across classrooms it becomes quite a different matter. Departmental and school-wide policy has to promote best practice, whilst giving teachers autonomy to make their own decisions. The strategies in this book have been applied across successful departments and each chapter suggests systems and structures that are effective, yet flexible. I hope that those of you who are middle and senior leaders will find ideas in this book that you can take forward to help implement change in your schools, whether that be a collaborative school-wide approach to teaching and learning or simply picking out and discussing ideas at department meetings. My advice would be to ensure teaching and learning occupies at least one agenda item at any subject meeting. Pick an idea and go with it!

The evidence base

There is a growing body of evidence-based research in the field of education which suggests that certain teaching strategies have a greater impact on student achievement than others. This research, despite some of its criticism, continues to change the way schools approach teaching and learning, professional development, curriculum design and school policy. Furthermore, evidence-based research substantiates the Five Components of Outstanding Learning and the positive impact they have on the achievement of learners. The principles of evidence-based teaching are the source for this practical guide and, within the pages of this book, I am confident you will find a wide variety of ideas, tools and strategies that will help you, no matter what your subject, make a difference to the quality of learning in your classroom.

At the start of each chapter, you will find a useful infographic that makes reference to some of the evidence-based research and its pertinence to the strategies within that section. This infographic directly relates to some of the most prevalent research and meta-analysis in the field of education – Marzano *et al.* (2001), Hattie (2009) and Higgins *et al.* (2014). Although the purpose of this book is not to pursue academic insight, making reference to the research and evidence gives justification to the strategies in each chapter and the experiential learning that formed them. Below is a brief summary of the research presented in this infographic:

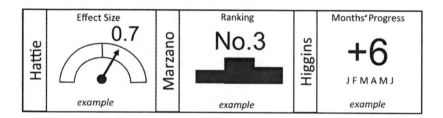

1. Hattie (2009) conducted a synthesis of over 800 meta-analyses relating to student achievement. Although it concluded that most educational strategies have a positive impact on student achievement, an effect size of 0.4 is considered average for educational research and, therefore, any approach with an effect size greater than 0.4 is particularly worthwhile.

2. Marzano *et al.* (2001) identified nine instructional strategies for classroom practice that maximise student performance. Where these notable nine strategies are linked to the content of a chapter, they are highlighted in the infographic.

3. The Teaching and Learning Toolkit produced by The Sutton Trust–Education Endowment Fund and written by Higgins *et al.* (2014) is an ongoing body of research into teaching and learning strategies. As of June 2014, the toolkit covered 34 topics, each summarised in terms of their average impact on attainment and measured in terms of additional months'

progress over the course of a year. For example, +3 would represent 3 months' additional progress on average where that method has been successfully applied.

The aim of this research is to help schools and teachers make informed decisions as to how their resources and energies should be deployed. From experience, the ideas within this book have been carefully selected, not only because they complement the research, but because they are particularly effective approaches to classroom practice.

How to use this book

The chapters of this book have been broken down into the five conditions for outstanding learning, with Chapter 1 focusing on how teachers can effectively plan lessons to achieve learning goals. Following each chapter, you will also find a useful list of 'Top tens' covering a range of issues. This book is designed to allow the busy teacher (sound familiar?) to quickly find an idea to meet their needs. The quick reference guide on page 7 identifies 24 categories, such as 'a way to stretch and challenge students' or 'a way to provide effective feedback' and cross-references these objectives against every idea in the book. So, when you're looking for a strategy to 'add a bit of fun to your lesson', just 'dip in' and pick out a tool that does just that.

Wherever possible, you will find ideas broken down into succinct chunks of information to make it easy to follow and apply in your own context. Each strategy starts with a brief overview that explains what is involved and how it works, followed by:

- *What to do* – a step-by-step approach to each strategy given in a series of bullet points;

- *Variations* – some ideas on how the strategy could be approached from different subjects and contexts;

- *Works well with* – highlights some of the others strategies within the book that might compliment the idea;

- *Teaching tip* – a few words of advice from experience to help you get it right.

You will also find free resources and support for many of the strategies explained in this book through my companion website: **www.essentialteachingandlearning.com.**

Chapter 1 takes a slightly different tack to the other five chapters as it offers a planning model to help teachers cover all aspects of an effective lesson. This chapter also explores ideas on how we can use data to inform and guide teaching and learning.

This book offers tons of helpful ideas and advice. However, this does not mean that picking an idea and imposing it on 10b3 English, period 1 Monday morning, will automatically be a success. Neither is a scattergun approach of throwing three to four ideas into a lesson likely to have the desired effect. Every teacher, class and student is different – what worked one day might not necessarily work the next. This is what makes our profession so interesting, exciting and often frustrating. An idea might not work the first time, or indeed the second, but as teachers we craft our trade and get better with practice. I hope that the readers of this book will choose those ideas that meet their needs then try them out, adapt and develop them to suit their own context and, in the spirit of collaborative learning, enthusiastically share those ideas with others.

At the time of writing this book, there is a lot of change and uncertainty in the UK education system. Whichever side of the political fence you sit on, it is easy to get distracted, worried or angry by these reforms. But no matter what these changes bring about, the fundamentals of what we do, as educators, stays the same. Consequently, writing this compendium of ideas has helped me, and I hope the readers of this book too, focus on the stuff that really matters and makes the biggest difference to student's lives – the quality of teaching and learning.

Referencing system

Page I want to find...

Key to statements:

(1) A good activity for a starter
(2) A way to encourage effective collaboration
(3) An effective revision exercise
(4) A way to get students reflecting on their learning and progress
(5) A way to encourage deeper thinking and decision making
(6) An active task to get your students moving
(7) An activity to encourage creativity
(8) A way to deliver and manage learning objectives
(9) A way to manage behaviour for learning in my lessons
(10) A way to praise and reward students
(11) A way to personalise and differentiate learning
(12) A way to stretch and challenge students
(13) A way to structure or a system for learning in my lessons
(14) A way to improve the quality of questioning
(15) A way to encourage student-led independent learning
(16) A way to share learning expectations
(17) A way to review learning and progress in my lessons
(18) A strategy to provide effective feedback to students
(19) A way to add a bit of fun to my lessons
(20) A way to encourage healthy competition in my lessons
(21) An effective assessment for learning strategy
(22) An effective use of ICT
(23) A way to build flexibility and choice into my lessons
(24) A good activity for a plenary

Page	Technique	(1)	(2)	(3)	(4)	(5)	(6)	(7)	(8)	(9)	(10)	(11)	(12)	(13)	(14)	(15)	(16)	(17)	(18)	(19)	(20)	(21)	(22)	(23)	(24)
199	A Dot Marks the Spot	✓			✓						✓			✓					✓			✓			
145	A Quick Response			✓								✓	✓		✓	✓			✓						
163	A Token Question												✓			✓	✓					✓			
152	Accelerated Learning Contracts												✓	✓		✓	✓					✓		✓	
177	AfL Dashboard				✓			✓	✓			✓			✓			✓				✓	✓	✓	
192	AfL Playing Cards		✓	✓	✓							✓						✓							✓
31	All-student Response Techniques					✓	✓			✓				✓		✓									
55	Always, Sometimes, Never				✓	✓					✓														✓
119	Answer Analyst (Learning Leaders)													✓											✓

(Continued)

(Continued)

	(1)	(2)	(3)	(4)	(5)	(6)	(7)	(8)	(9)	(10)	(11)	(12)	(13)	(14)	(15)	(16)	(17)	(18)	(19)	(20)	(21)	(22)	(23)	(24)
135 Ask the Teacher	✓	✓												✓										
108 Assume Conformity		✓							✓															
97 Auction House			✓		✓													✓				✓		
201 Automated Marking	✓																							
175 Bad Answers				✓												✓		✓						
35 Baseline Sorting						✓					✓								✓	✓	✓			✓
82 Blankety Blank	✓					✓	✓					✓							✓	✓				✓
147 Bloom's Challenge Wall		✓		✓	✓	✓		✓					✓		✓	✓								✓
75 Board of Revision											✓	✓									✓			
96 Bowling	✓✓																							
95 Catch the Bus										✓														
39 Celebrate Success						✓			✓		✓	✓	✓		✓		✓		✓	✓			✓	✓
149 Challenge Corner			✓								✓				✓	✓	✓						✓	
150 Challenge Envelope																							✓	
175 Checklists																								
182 Checkpoint It (Review Wheel)				✓									✓									✓		✓
63 Choice																								
170 Chunking		✓																						
86 Cluedo																								
202 Comment Keys		✓✓	✓	✓	✓		✓	✓	✓		✓		✓		✓				✓	✓	✓	✓	✓✓	✓
125 Composite Answers		✓✓		✓✓	✓✓						✓		✓✓		✓✓	✓			✓		✓✓		✓✓	✓✓
88 Comprehension Cranium																								
64 Conditions for Learning Model	✓																							
36 Confidence Levels				✓✓	✓				✓		✓	✓			✓				✓					
59 Connect Four	✓			✓																				
47 Consider All Possibilities																								
109 Consistency		✓	✓	✓	✓	✓			✓									✓				✓	✓	
138 Contributing Ideas and Opinions Digitally							✓✓				✓				✓								✓✓	
133 Creativity Carousel		✓✓✓	✓	✓	✓							✓✓✓	✓✓					✓	✓	✓		✓	✓✓	
48 Creativity Wheel, The		✓✓✓										✓✓✓	✓										✓	
171 Cultural Reference Buddies (EAL)			✓		✓✓																			
132 Debates				✓✓	✓✓								✓✓		✓				✓	✓	✓		✓	
197 Delayed Grading																								
76 Diamond 9s	✓	✓		✓✓															✓	✓	✓✓	✓	✓	✓

117 Dictionary Dude (Learning Leaders)
140 Digital Quizzes
138 Digital Tools for Curating
136 Digital Tools to Flip the Classroom
120 Disposition Doctor (Learning Leaders)
82 Dominoes
172 Down Time (EAL)
90 Dream Pictures
40 Effort Ranking
169 Engaging Learning Styles
188 Examining the Exam
51 Exit Signs
123 Expert Groups
181 Explain It (Review Wheel)
69 Exploded Venn, The
46 Favourite Things
193 Feedback Grids
200 Feedback Keys
189 Five for Five
121 Five Group Roles
201 Focused Feedback
68 Force-field Analysis
196 Four-part Marking Framework
131 Four-way Worksheets
198 Framing Feedback
95 Freeze Frame
118 Go Get Googler (Learning Leaders)
155 Going SOLO with Baseball
197 Green Pen of Growth
72 Group work Pie Chart
87 Guess Who Quotes
169 Half-finished Notes

	(1)	(2)	(3)	(4)	(5)	(6)	(7)	(8)	(9)	(10)	(11)	(12)	(13)	(14)	(15)	(16)	(17)	(18)	(19)	(20)	(21)	(22)	(23)	(24)
102 Happy Snappers										✓				✓		✓						✓		✓
57 Hexlearning	✓	✓			✓		✓								✓								✓	
182 Hinge Questions	✓		✓								✓			✓	✓		✓				✓	✓		
200 Home Peer Marking		✓										✓												
137 Hosting a Virtual Classroom		✓	✓	✓	✓				✓					✓								✓		
29 Hot Questions				✓	✓		✓								✓									✓
109 Ignoring Secondary Behaviour				✓	✓		✓		✓			✓	✓		✓					✓			✓	✓
71 In and Out Box, The				✓					✓							✓		✓			✓			
101 In the News	✓			✓	✓				✓				✓											
157 Independent Learning Projects																				✓				
120 Information Inquisition (Learning Leaders)											✓		✓		✓						✓			
37 Information-rich Seating Plans							✓	✓	✓		✓		✓	✓	✓		✓		✓	✓		✓	✓	✓
108 Instructional Cues											✓													
138 Interacting with Digital Content											✓		✓					✓	✓					
154 Interest Inventories							✓		✓		✓												✓	✓
197 Just Comment	✓																							
201 Just Grade																								
85 Justification Jenga																								
158 Lessons that Flow							✓	✓				✓	✓	✓	✓							✓		✓
170 Live Modelling	✓		✓	✓	✓			✓																
166 Making a Statement												✓		✓	✓		✓					✓		✓
140 Managing Projects Online	✓		✓	✓																				
69 Mandala Diagrams	✓		✓	✓																				
181 Map It (Review Wheel)					✓	✓	✓					✓		✓	✓	✓				✓				✓
201 Margin Marking				✓																				
113 Maslow in the Classroom	✓		✓	✓	✓		✓								✓		✓							✓
71 Matrix, The	✓										✓	✓	✓		✓	✓		✓	✓	✓				✓
181 MCQ It (Review Wheel)	✓	✓	✓	✓	✓																			
198 Medal and a Mission		✓											✓											
108 Meet and Greet	✓				✓	✓	✓							✓		✓		✓	✓	✓		✓		✓
92 Memory Runs	✓	✓					✓				✓													
68 Mind Maps	✓	✓	✓		✓																			
31 No Hands Techniques																					✓			
172 Note-taking (EAL)	✓										✓													
104 Now That's What I Call...					✓		✓				✓		✓					✓	✓			✓		✓

Page	Entry
117	Objectives Overseer (Learning Leaders)
201	One to Mark
141	Online Sources of Inspiration
97	Opinion Line
109	Partial Agreement
134	Pass the Parcel Essays
108	Pause and Proximity
200	Peer Marking
191	Peer Ordering
121	Peer Praiser (Learning Leaders)
169	Picture Clues
184	Picture, Question, Answer (PQA)
58	Picture Wall
21	Planning for Progress
50	Plenary Dice
108	Positive Instruction
181	Post It (Review Wheel)
98	Post-it On
197	Pre-grading
34	Progress Flight Paths
171	Progress Not Attainment (EAL)
39	Progress Wall Charts
186	Pupil Principal Examiners
198	Purple Pen of Progress
54	Question Box
55	Question Matrix, The
119	Question Qualifier (Learning Leaders)
31	Question Techniques for Variety
17	Questions for Planning Differentiation
166	Questions that FLOW
183	Questions under the Chair
171	Quick Turnaround Homework

(Continued)

(Continued)

	(1)	(2)	(3)	(4)	(5)	(6)	(7)	(8)	(9)	(10)	(11)	(12)	(13)	(14)	(15)	(16)	(17)	(18)	(19)	(20)	(21)	(22)	(23)	(24)
128 Quiz Quiz Trade	✓	✓	✓			✓														✓				✓
193 RAG Reflections		✓		✓			✓										✓					✓		✓
109 Repair and Rebuild										✓					✓						✓			✓
181 Report It (Review Wheel)	✓		✓	✓		✓			✓	✓					✓					✓		✓		✓
93 Revision Football																								
78 Safe		✓						✓				✓				✓	✓	✓	✓				✓	✓
170 Scaffolding	✓	✓				✓			✓	✓	✓	✓	✓	✓	✓	✓			✓		✓	✓		✓
151 Secret Mission	✓																							
140 Sharing Resources Digitally	✓	✓																						
171 Short Homework (EAL)									✓	✓	✓	✓	✓	✓	✓	✓		✓	✓					
199 Signed For											✓													
127 Silent Galleries	✓			✓	✓	✓			✓															
61 Six Learning Junctions, The	✓			✓		✓			✓	✓			✓		✓	✓					✓			
66 Skills Icons	✓			✓																				
120 Skills Selector (Learning Leaders)	✓																							
137 Social Networks for Learning	✓	✓	✓									✓	✓		✓							✓	✓	
52 Socratic Plenary, The	✓	✓			✓			✓					✓	✓	✓									✓
164 Solve It			✓		✓										✓									
103 Special Guest	✓																					✓		
69 Spectrum, The	✓	✓	✓			✓	✓		✓	✓	✓				✓	✓		✓	✓	✓				✓
129 Speed Dating	✓	✓	✓			✓																		
38 Spiky Kids	✓																							
100 Splat	✓	✓									✓					✓		✓						
200 Student Model Answers	✓			✓						✓	✓	✓		✓	✓	✓		✓		✓		✓		
125 Student Tutors				✓			✓		✓	✓	✓				✓	✓		✓						
187 Summative Sound Bites			✓	✓			✓		✓		✓													
159 Taking the Credit	✓																						✓	
170 Talking and Thinking Before Inking																								
176 Talking Tins																							✓	
124 Talking Tokens	✓	✓		✓					✓	✓	✓	✓	✓		✓	✓			✓	✓	✓	✓	✓	
160 Targeted Objectives	✓				✓																			
199 Targets at the Top		✓		✓	✓					✓	✓	✓												
162 Ten Minute Taste for Teaching	✓	✓	✓	✓			✓		✓		✓	✓	✓		✓						✓	✓	✓	✓
100 Ten Minutes of TED	✓	✓		✓											✓							✓	✓	

91	Ten-word Challenge
89	Text Trivia
120	The Count (Learning Leaders)
36	The Exit Pass
94	The Writing's on the Window
67	Thinking Word Cards
152	Thinking Extension
178	Thinking Hats Writing Frames
128	Think–Pair–Square–Share
161	Thoughts and Crosses
71	Three Buckets, The
185	Three to Go
117	Time Technician (Learning Leaders)
85	Timed Talking
83	Top Trumps
99	Trading Choices
181	Traffic Light It (Review Wheel)
41	Trend Spotting
102	Tweet It (Review Wheel)
176	Visualisers
105	Voiceover
15	We Are Learning. . . So That. . .
79	Wildcard Quizzes
119	Wonder Worder (Learning Leaders)
39	Word Banks
105	X Factor Songs

A plan for learning

As trainee teachers, we spent hours and hours planning lessons, and for most teachers planning lessons and schemes of learning takes a considerable chunk of our working week. In fact, the Department for Education's Teachers' Workload Diary Survey 2013 found that a typical working week for a secondary school classroom teacher equated to 55.7 hours – of which, 19.6 are spent teaching. The survey also showed that planning, preparation and assessment time contributed 8.5 of these hours. This would suggest that for every hour of teaching the average classroom teacher spends approximately 26 minutes planning. Whilst the focus of this book is predominantly about what goes on in the classroom, it seems reasonable to devote some attention to this crucial part of our practice. Therefore, the purpose of this chapter is to outline a simple and efficient structure for planning outstanding lessons that prompts questions to help teachers make important decisions about teaching and learning.

It was Dwight D. Eisenhower who said 'plans are nothing; planning is everything' and this is as true of lesson planning as it is of anything else. A hundred different things can happen in a lesson that can make even the most detailed plan obsolete before the starter activity is over. However, the real benefits of lesson plans come from the thinking that goes on through the planning process and the resulting decisions we make. On page 16, you will find a lesson planning template that we will refer to as The Five-Part Lesson Plan. Each phase covers a key component of planning and on one page provides a series of questions and visual prompts to ensure teachers consider those aspects that contribute towards outstanding lessons. Below is an explanation of The Five-Part Lesson Plan and, starting on page 22, you will find three examples of planning by three different teachers who have used this framework to prompt their own ideas. These lesson plans, along with the template, can be downloaded from the website.

The Five-Part Lesson Plan

The Five-Part Lesson Plan is designed to be conducive to doodling and simple to use (Figure 1.1). Although each part is numbered, the planning process is seldom linear. For example, an idea for an activity could easily be formed before we consider how we might assess the learning, how we might differentiate it or even before we have decided on the lesson objectives. There is no correct order, so long as each part is given due consideration. Whilst using The Five-Part Lesson Plan is no guarantee that your lesson will be outstanding, the planning and thought that goes into it will be.

Part 1: Purpose

Step one in The Five-Part Lesson Plan is to consider the purpose and direction of the lesson. Most commonly referred to as the objectives and outcomes. As teachers, we use lesson objectives and outcomes because it gives direction to our lessons, helps teachers and students measure progress and, if done correctly, helps engage and motivate students.

The first box in the top left corner refers to the 'big picture', in other words, where we are, where we have come from and where we are going. Whereas lesson objectives may refer more to the purpose and goals of a particular lesson, the big picture is about framing the lesson in the context of the course, unit or scheme of learning. This is important because students like to see a holistic picture of their learning in order to understand how each lesson and new piece of information contributes towards the grand design. It might not be necessary, or always appropriate, to make this explicit during every lesson, but it is important that students get to checkpoint their learning on a regular basis. One common way to share this information with students is through a table of contents in the form of a checklist that students can use to monitor their progress and use as a guide to organise their revision. Other techniques might involve graphic organisers such as mind maps, timelines or honeycombs (see Hexlearning, page 57) to communicate the course content. The use of these techniques and other graphical organisers is covered at length in Chapter 2.

There are many ways to form and share objectives with students. Some teachers might define two to three objectives with measurable outcomes; some might set an objective as a big question and others may adopt the 'all, most, some' approach to objective setting, but for me this has always seemed a bit deterministic. The approach I have settled on is simple, clear and helps us pre-empt questions such as 'why are we learning this?' or the dreaded 'when will I need. . .?'

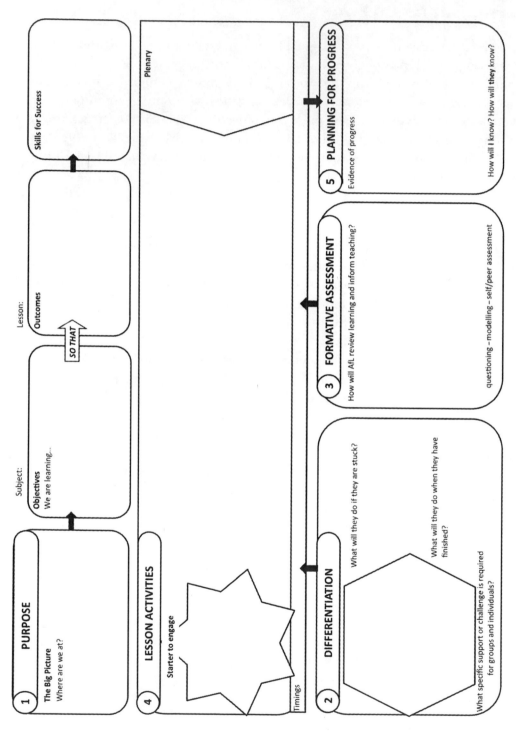

Figure 1.1 The Five-Part Lesson Plan

Furthermore, this approach helps teachers tie their objectives into the learning outcomes. I first came across this idea in Zoe Elder's excellent Full On Learning blog.[1] The approach is quite straightforward and requires the use of a simple connective – so that – to link the lesson objectives to the learning outcomes. The merits of this approach is that it gets teachers to think about the *why* behind the lesson objective and makes the purpose explicit to students. See some examples of effective objective setting in the sample lesson plans starting on page 22.

There are times when the 'so that' might lead to an outcome that is difficult to measure. However, if your intention is to achieve a more explicit or tangible outcome, a further stem could be added, such as 'we will know because. . .'. This then gives us something we can directly use to assess students' progress throughout the lesson.

The final box under the Purpose section of the planning template leaves space to consider 'skills for success'. The purpose of this prompt is to encourage teachers to consider any skills, dispositions or characteristics that are key to success during that lesson. This will be linked to the activities that students take part in during that lesson. For example, if the lesson requires students to analyse and evaluate a situation based on different people's perspectives, then a key 'skill for success' might be their ability to empathise. Highlighting 'empathy' as a key disposition will give a class the opportunity to discuss what it means in the context of their learning and how they might go about modelling it. Similarly, a lesson that involves significant group work might denote teamwork as a key skill, leading to a class discussion on what effective teamwork might look like (see sample lesson plan in Figure 1.4). The purpose of highlighting such skills with students is to encourage them to think about their own learning, the way they interact with others and how they conduct themselves during the lesson. Furthermore, if your school has a values system or promotes the development of a set of skills for learning then this is an opportunity to build this into your day-to-day planning. This section can also be used to highlight important subject-related skills (see sample lesson plan in Figure 1.3). This idea of identifying 'skills for success' supports the concept of split-screen thinking outlined by Claxton (2002) as it encourages students to build learning capacity – the skills and dispositions that are key to life-long learning. We explore these further in Chapter 2.

Part 2: Differentiation

Differentiating lessons is about considering the needs of different individuals and groups of learners, and for many is one of the most challenging aspects of teaching. Chapter 3 considers how we can meet the different needs of our students through providing the right balance of challenge and support and, in doing so, successfully differentiate lessons.

The hexagonal box in the bottom left of the template can be used to divide your class into distinctive groups or identify specific students who have unique needs (see sample lesson plan in Figure 1.2). In particular, planning for students with special educational needs is non-negotiable – they should always be catered for in the planning of a lesson. Apart from these individuals, it is likely that you might identify high-ability students and lower-ability students as the ones who require additional challenge or support. Chapter 5 is dedicated to strategies that can help teachers differentiate their lessons at both ends of the spectrum and support the varying needs of learners. Although we might make specific plans for certain individuals or groups of learners, it is true that the most effective differentiation takes place not through the extension work or scaffolding we put in place, but through the dialogue, marking of work and subsequent feedback we give. Therefore, much of what we do to differentiate learning is not explicitly planned for lesson by lesson. Nevertheless, we should always try to make provisions for students who will make progress at different speeds. Consequently, here are two questions that are always useful to consider when planning for differentiation:

1.   What will students do when they have finished?

2.   What will students do when they are stuck?

The purpose of the first question is to ensure all students are appropriately challenged. Students should be able to move on to more challenging tasks and this is commonly achieved through an extension activity, which if it is to be successful should always avoid activities that are 'more of the same'. The second question is there as a prompt to make us think about how we can support students when they 'get stuck'. For example, directing students to various sources of support to overcome an obstacle. The answer to these questions might not be unique for each task or lesson, as some teachers might choose to use a standard approach in answering these questions that they expect all students to adopt whilst in their lesson. These approaches are often linked to a culture of independence where students are encouraged to take responsibility for their own learning. For example, the expectation that all students will get out a dictionary when they are unsure of a spelling or give themselves the 'green light' to move on to more challenging tasks when they feel they are ready to do so. Ideas such as Solve It (page 164) and Challenge Corner (page 149) are both useful strategies that can build independence if used consistently.

Part 3: Formative assessment

As Black and Wiliam discovered back in 1998, where assessment for learning is effectively implemented, it raises the standard of achievement across the board. Although we may plan to use summative assessment during lessons, the purpose of this section is to help teachers plan how they might use formative assessment tools as part of the learning process. This includes the way we share the learning expectations, questioning strategies, self- and peer-assessment and teacher feedback. Assessment for learning is therefore the barometer we use to measure learning gains in order to inform and modify our teaching.

In addition to the guiding work of Black and Wiliam (1998) and Black *et al.* (2002), assessment for learning, in its various forms, ranks amongst the top teaching methods in all the evidence-based research for improving student attainment. This alone justifies its worthiness on any lesson planning form and why Chapter 6 has been dedicated to the topic, where you will find a variety of practical ideas.

Questioning is the most simple yet effective tool we have for formative assessment. Questioning techniques are covered in Chapter 5 as a strategy for differentiation and as a formative assessment strategy in Chapter 6. It might seem odd to explicitly plan our use of questions during a lesson; possibly because questioning is a skill we develop as teachers, like driving a car or tying a shoelace – it's something we just do and often don't even think about it. Nevertheless, we can make a conscious effort to ask better questions and encourage our students to do the same. Techniques such as Questions that FLOW (page 166), Hinge Questions (page 182), Review Wheel (page 180) or Assessment Statements (page 167) allow us to differentiate assessment and measure progress. Even if we don't plan to use a particular approach to questioning, this part of the lesson plan can be used to make a note of a few good questions that could prompt thinking and guide discussion. Consequently, Part 3 of the planning framework offers teachers an opportunity to plan their lessons around good questions, and not just activities (see sample lesson plan in Figure 1.4).

In Chapter 6, you will also find a wide range of ideas to carry out self- and peer-assessments and share the learning expectations, as well as strategies for quick learning reviews, sometimes referred to as the 'mini plenary'. These can all be used to great effect to guide the learning process, although it is important to use them with caution. I have observed lessons where the proceedings are stopped every few minutes so that the learning could be reviewed with a 'mini plenary'. In this instance, formative assessment was more a hindrance than a tool to inform and guide teaching and learning. We must remember that there is nothing wrong with letting students get on with it when they are learning. There is a time in every lesson for these strategies, but they should all be used in the right measure. When formative assessment is used correctly, it motivates students and builds their self-esteem, leading to a culture of success where all can achieve.

Part 4: Lesson activities

The fourth stage of the process is to plan for the resources and activities that will support students in their learning and help them achieve the lesson objectives. As you would expect, the first part of the lesson involves what has become known as the starter activity.

A pre-starter or early bird activity is mainly used to settle and focus students as they arrive at your lesson. They have no other purpose, unlike a starter, which will be used to assess prior knowledge and/or engage students in the topic being learnt. The great thing about using a starter activity to assess students' entry level is that it gives us a clear point at which to measure progress over the course of the lesson. For example, helping students demonstrate that they can do something at the end of a lesson that they could not at the start. One way to do this is to link the starter activity to the plenary through strategies such as Picture Wall (page 58) or getting students to evaluate a statement that you posed at the start of the lesson. Starters can also be a great opportunity to get your class to guess the purpose of the lesson. Simply project a picture, write a word on the whiteboard or play a piece of music that relates to the topic of the lesson. Setting your lesson up as a bit of a mystery is often a nice way to begin as it creates a 'hook' to engage students.

At the opposite end of the activities box, we have a space to plan our plenary. The plenary should be an opportunity to recap and reflect on progress by returning to the lesson objectives and should aim to consolidate the learning that has taken place. Having said this, I do not believe that a plenary has to be a discrete planned activity that takes place at the end of the lesson. Having a rigid end point can often be counterproductive. The last thing we want to do is bolt on an activity that has little relevance to the learning that has taken place. Instead, what we should aim for is a meaningful end to the lesson that informs both teachers and students about the learning that has taken place. As teachers, we are then appropriately placed to make plans for future lessons.

The main body of a lesson is then formed by the activities that we plan and facilitate. The formative assessment strategies planned in Part 3 will also feed into Part 4 to help teachers review the learning that takes place so to guide your teaching. Whether you are planning group activities, student presentations, active games or whole-class discussions, I am sure you will find something within this book that fits the bill.

Part 5: Planning for progress

Part 5 of the planning template has been included to encourage teachers to think about progression and how they can make this visible to their students. Of course, this may have already been considered when deciding on the lesson objectives, formative assessment strategies and the plenary, as each of these can demonstrate progress and encourage students to be active responsible learners. However, it is still worth thinking about how this progress can be evidenced through students' work, demonstrations or simply the responding to questions.

The two questions inside the box, 'How will I know?' and 'How will they know?', prompt us to consider where there might be opportunities to provide feedback and record evidence. For example, here we might identify a piece of work that we intend to mark, level and provide feedback to students. This might also provide an opportunity for students to respond to your feedback and make the necessary improvements. Our marking can directly feed into our planning and this dialogue between teachers and students is an excellent record of progress.

Often progress is observational; it is not always possible or appropriate to collect hard evidence. After all, the purpose of the lesson is learning and not collecting evidence. Alternatively, this box can be used to make observations and notes at the end of your lesson in order to inform future planning. Notes on individual students, the success of an activity or perhaps an area you want to recover in your next lesson are all worthwhile and will help you make the most of your next lesson (see sample lesson plan in Figure 1.4).

A final word on planning lessons

The purpose of this planning template is to act as an aid that prompts teachers to think about those aspects of teaching that lead to effective lessons. Take the bits you like, the bits that work for you and your subject and ignore the rest. There is nothing worse than a lesson where the teacher has tried to cram everything in, often for the sake of an observer. In these circumstances, the lesson will always be driven by the activities and the clock, instead of the learning. It's great if you can pull it off, but this is never the reality of day-to-day practice. We can't plan for everything and often things don't work out as we planned. However, if we cover the important aspects of teaching and learning, the result will, more often than not, be an effective lesson.

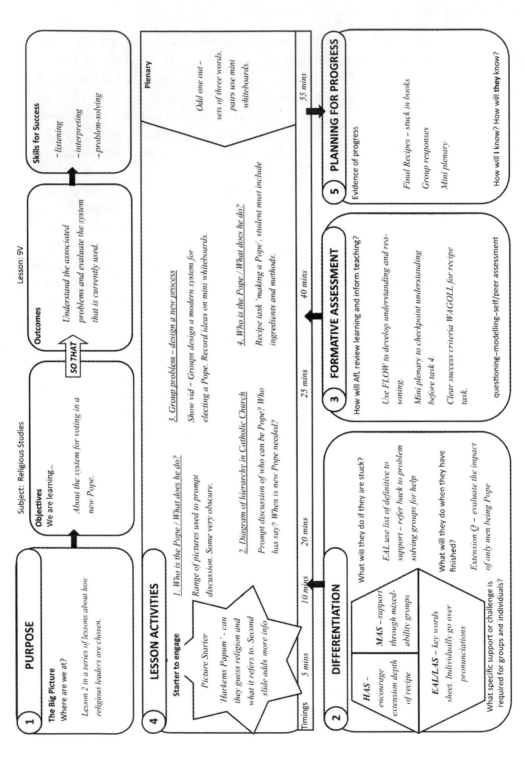

Figure 1.2 Sample lesson plan 1

Planning in practice

Sample lesson 1: Religious Studies (Picking a Pope)

Contributed by Louise Cline

This lesson is preceded by two lessons looking at how Buddhists identify reincarnated Lamas and is followed by looking at how Coptic Christians choose their Pope. The aim of the first lesson is for pupils to get a clear understanding of the process whereby Catholics choose their Pope.

The lesson is designed to impart quite a lot of background knowledge to students to help inform their decisions but also to get them to solve some of the problems associated with the process themselves. The starter is designed to get pupils to use their knowledge from other lessons to identify the religion/denomination. In history, they look at the reformation so they know that the Catholic Church uses Latin and they may see that 'Papum' is a bit like the word 'Pope'. The first few parts of the lesson give quite a lot of detail but this is needed for pupils to compete the 'recipe' task successfully. The problem-solving exercise is not about pupils getting the right answers, just about them being able to give ideas with reasoning. The recipe task is a fun way of getting pupils to review their learning. They have a list of words that they must include in either their ingredients or method. Getting pupils to record their ideas in this format gets them to think about how to present the process simply, but also challenges their thinking, e.g. can an ingredient be a non-physical thing?

When teaching the lesson, I found that many students wanted to add extra bits which you often found in recipes, e.g. preparation time, which showed real creativity. The plenary is designed to be accessed by all students. The more able may come up with more creative suggestions but all can take part and feel a sense of achievement.

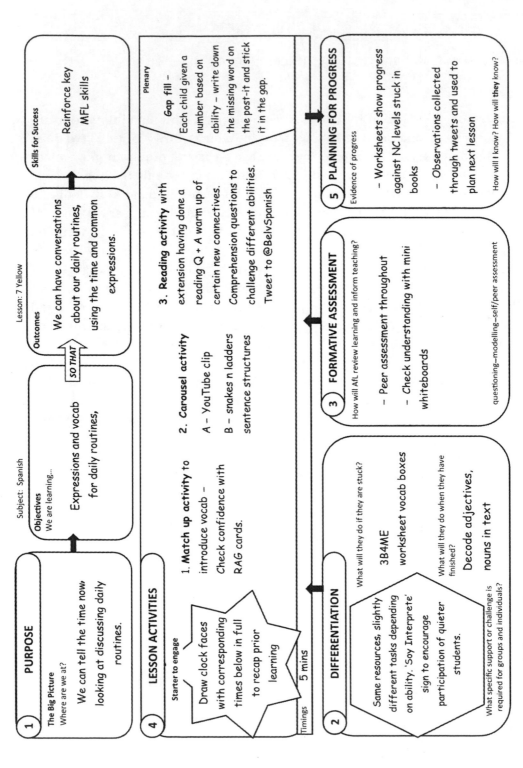

Figure 1.3 Sample lesson plan 2

Subject: Spanish   Lesson: 7 Yellow

1 PURPOSE

The Big Picture
Where are we at?

We can tell the time now looking at discussing daily routines.

Objectives
We are learning...

Expressions and vocab for daily routines,

SO THAT

Outcomes

We can have conversations about our daily routines, using the time and common expressions.

Skills for Success

Reinforce key MFL skills

4 LESSON ACTIVITIES

Starter to engage

Draw clock faces with corresponding times below in full to recap prior learning

Timings   5 mins

1. **Match up activity** to introduce vocab –

Check confidence with RAG cards.

2. **Carousel activity**

A – YouTube clip

B – snakes n ladders sentence structures

3. **Reading activity** with extension having done a reading Q + A warm up of certain new connectives. Comprehension questions to challenge different abilities.
Tweet to @BelvSpanish

Plenary

Gap fill –
Each child given a number based on ability – write down the missing word on the post-it and stick it in the gap.

2 DIFFERENTIATION

What will they do if they are stuck?

3B4ME
worksheet vocab boxes

What will they do when they have finished?

Decode adjectives, nouns in text

What specific support or challenge is required for groups and individuals?

Some resources, slightly different tasks depending on ability. 'Soy Interprete' sign to encourage participation of quieter students.

3 FORMATIVE ASSESSMENT

How will AfL review learning and inform teaching?

- Peer assessment throughout

- Check understanding with mini whiteboards

questioning–modelling–self/peer assessment

5 PLANNING FOR PROGRESS

Evidence of progress

- Worksheets show progress against NC levels stuck in books

- Observations collected through tweets and used to plan next lesson

How will I know? How will they know?

Sample lesson 2: Spanish (Daily Routine)

Contributed by Sean McGovern

Year 7 Yellow have just completed learning how to tell the time, so we are moving on to study daily routine to be able to use this in conjunction with time. The students have studied the present tense of regular verbs, but we will be learning the present time of reflexive verbs through implicit grammatical teaching. The class members' target levels range between 4a and 4c in French following recent assessments. Some girls achieved Level 5 in speaking assessment.

In this lesson we are learning a lot of content through fun and games-style activities, whilst building on and applying previously learnt material. The lesson follows a sequence of teaching the time, to then be able to purposefully use the time when describing their own daily routine.

This lesson incorporates all four skills of the MFL framework: listening, reading, speaking and writing. Furthermore, the activities nurture the social skills of teamwork and independent learning, along with problem-solving. The difficulty of the material works its way up the NC levels, from implicit grammatical teaching of the reflexive present tense to eventually producing a Level 5 writing piece.

In my lessons, there is a culture of visiting the 'Reflection Wheel' or being a 'Learning Leader'. 'Review Wheel' gives them a number of different ways to reflect on their learning at any point of the lesson through mind maps, 30-second summaries, tweeting and a range of other strategies.

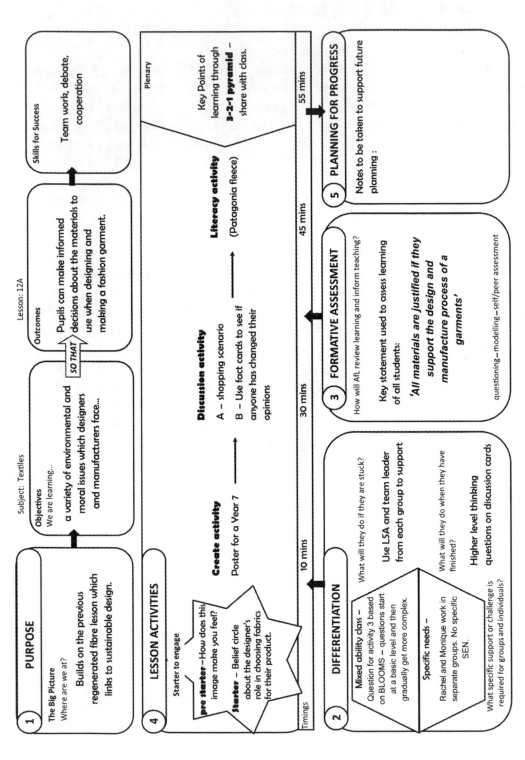

Subject: Textiles   Lesson: 12A

1 PURPOSE

The Big Picture
Where are we at?

Builds on the previous regenerated fibre lesson which links to sustainable design.

Objectives
We are learning…

a variety of environmental and moral issues which designers and manufacturers face…

SO THAT

Outcomes

Pupils can make informed decisions about the materials to use when designing and making a fashion garment.

Skills for Success

Team work, debate, cooperation

4 LESSON ACTIVITIES

Starter to engage

pre starter – How does this image make you feel?

Starter – Belief circle about the designer's role in choosing fabrics for their product.

Create activity
Poster for a Year 7

Discussion activity

A – shopping scenario

B – Use fact cards to see if anyone has changed their opinions

Literacy activity
(Patagonia fleece)

Plenary

Key Points of learning through
3–2–1 pyramid – share with class.

Timings   10 mins   30 mins   45 mins   55 mins

2 DIFFERENTIATION

Mixed ability class – Question for activity 3 based on BLOOMS – questions start at a basic level and then gradually get more complex.

Specific needs –
Rachel and Monique work in separate groups. No specific SEN.

What specific support or challenge is required for groups and individuals?

What will they do if they are stuck?

Use LSA and team leader from each group to support

What will they do when they have finished?

Higher level thinking questions on discussion cards

3 FORMATIVE ASSESSMENT

How will AfL review learning and inform teaching?

Key statement used to assess learning of all students:

'All materials are justified if they support the design and manufacture process of a garments'

questioning – modelling – self/peer assessment

5 PLANNING FOR PROGRESS

Notes to be taken to support future planning :

Figure 1.4   Sample lesson plan 3

Sample lesson 3: Design Technology (Environmental Issues in Design)

Contributed by Leander Jones

The lesson brings two of the main aspects of textiles design together: choosing the correct materials for a product and considering environmental and moral issues that designers may face when designing and manufacturing. The lesson starts with a pre-starter activity. The pre-starter leads directly into the objectives and the starter activity. The starter activity is a 'belief circle', which enables all pupils to make a range of personal judgements straight away. The classroom teacher can choose who will discuss their ideas and in some cases the more confident pupils will offer their opinions. The main lesson activities consist of three separate sections.

- *Creative task*: Students read information on regenerated fibres then produce a colourful bold poster, explaining what regenerated fibres are to a pupil in Year 7.

- *Discussion task*: (Part 1) Students imagine they are going shopping. They must individually choose one fashion item from each pair of products that they would like to buy and must write their choice on a piece of paper. Explain which products they chose and why, and what helped them to make their decision. (Part 2) Team leader to open the envelope and take out the cards. Ask pupils to read the information on the cards. Think and discuss. Would anybody change their opinions on what they bought?

- *Literacy task*: Team leader to read the main case study on Patagonia fleece to group. Discuss the BLOOMS questions given as a group, and then answer the questions on an individual basis.

The plenary enables pupils to interact with other members of the class who were not in their original groups. They can walk around and share their questions and answers with others. The homework consolidates their learning in class and enables the pupils to self-assess their questions to activity 3.

An answer to questioning

Throughout this book, you will find many teaching and learning strategies which, in essence, involve different ways of asking questions. As teachers we ask a lot of questions for a number of different reasons. In fact, research suggests that between 35 and 50 per cent of teachers' instructional time is spent doing just that. Although questioning does not command its own chapter, the principles of effective questioning permeate every part of this book. So, at this point it makes sense to lay down a few ground rules and consider some of the key questions about these instructional cues.

What types of questions should we ask?

The types of questions we use can be classified into a range of categories, but the general purpose of most questions is to test knowledge and probe understanding. It is an oft-quoted fact that a considerably smaller percentage of the questions teachers ask are of a higher cognitive nature (open-ended, evaluative or inferential) compared to lower cognitive questions (closed and factual) (see Figure 1.5). Wilen (1991) provides a summary of various studies on teacher questioning to prove this point. Furthermore, a literary review by Cotton (1998) also confirms this balance. These are initially worrying statistics as we all recognise the importance of asking higher-order questions in order to develop higher-order thinking and deeper understanding in our students. Nevertheless, Cotton (1998: 4) also concludes that 'higher cognitive questions are not categorically better than lower cognitive questions in eliciting higher level responses or in promoting learning gains'.

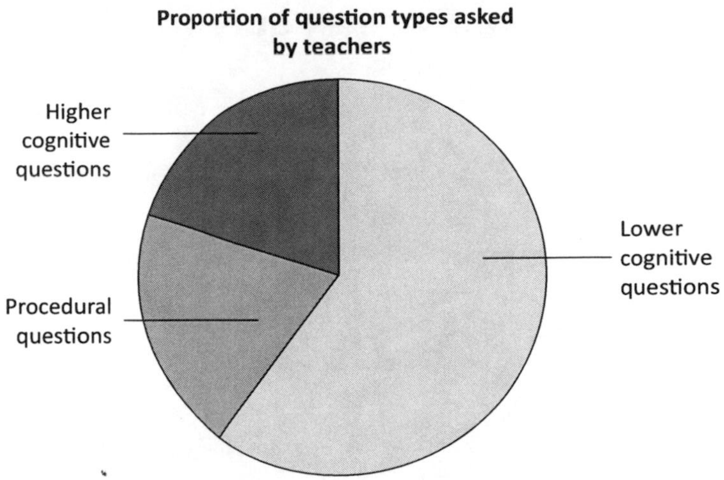

**Proportion of question types asked
by teachers**

Figure 1.5 Proportion of question types asked by teachers

**Although more value is placed on higher-order questions, it is important
that we use a mixture of both in the classroom.**

As teachers we can build on the lower-order questions we use to probe students'
understanding and progress to higher-order strategies. We can encourage this by
using Bloom's taxonomy as a prompt or incorporating what I call 'hot questions'
such as:

- What do you think?

- Why do you think that?

- How do you know?

- Do you all agree?

- Do you have a reason?

- Is there another way?

- Can you be sure?

- What is your evidence?

Strategies such as Socratic Questioning (page 52) or the Plenary Dice (page 50) are
other mechanisms that encourage reflection and deeper learning.

How should we ask questions?

The most common approach used by teachers when questioning students is still the 'hands up' approach, despite its obvious drawbacks. The only thing worse than the child sat daydreaming at the back of the class because they have been able to opt out of the lesson is the frustrated and demoralised student in the other corner who patiently waits to be picked. Even a more direct approach, such as randomly selecting students, only solves one of these issues and other evidence suggests that using too many questions of a similar style can leave students disengaged.

We need to use a variety of styles that engage the whole class and elicit responses from all students.

No hands techniques	
Lollipop sticks	Place student names on tongue depressors, place in a cup and randomly select a name. Coloured sticks can be used to target different types of students.
Random name generators	There are a wide variety of ICT solutions to help teachers randomly select students to target questions.
Volunteers and victims	Students are chosen to answer a question and asked to choose a peer to answer a follow-up question, give an opinion, offer an alternative or support the initial student in answering the question.

All-student response techniques	
Mini dry-wipe boards	All students write down their answers and reveal on the count of 3-2-1.
MCQ cue cards	Students can respond to any multiple-choice question by holding up a corresponding answer card (ABCD or RAG).
Post-it note wall	All students write an answer on a post-it and stick to the wall. Teacher has time to ponder each response, respond to interesting answers and assess the whole class.
Quizzing software	There are different types of web-based quizzing software that can be used to collect and collate responses from the whole class via a smartphone or similar device.

Question techniques to add variety	
Big questions	Framing the lesson objectives as an overarching question.
MCQs	*'What makes the best conductor?* *A. Metal* *B. Plastic* *C. Wood* *D. Cotton'*
Points of view	*'Should men and women be considered equal in every aspect?'*
Discussing statements	*'A person who does lots of exercise is healthy.'*
Odd one out	*'Which is the odd one out and why?'* or *'what is the difference between. . .?'*
Ordering, sorting and prioritising	*'Order these numbers from smallest to largest* *0.12 0.012 0.102 0.002 0.009'*
Answer first	*'The answer is 180. What could be the question?'*

How much wait time should we give before taking answers?

The headline statistic here is that teachers typically allow an average wait time of one second or less. Cotton goes on to suggest that around three seconds is the optimal amount of wait time for most types of question, but engagement in higher-order questions increases the longer students are given.

What if they don't know the answer or answer incorrectly?

We all want to build supportive and safe learning environments where every child can flourish. This was summarised by the motto of David Hudson, my previous headteacher: 'high challenge, low fear'. Unfortunately our hard work sometimes comes crashing down when a student is seen to be a failure because they don't know the answer to the question they were asked (another reason why we might be tempted to slip back into 'hands up' mode). It is an art form that teachers develop to draw the positives out of a wrong answer. How we deal with these moments can be the difference between improving a student's understanding and completely turning them off. As teachers we should be looking for wrong answers all the time, as they identify gaps in knowledge and show us where new opportunities for learning exist.

We need to build in mechanisms that give students time to think and engage with the question properly and access them at various levels. We need to reduce students' fear of being wrong.

When students raise their hand to answer a question, the temptation is to accept an answer from a student in your eye line. Simply waiting for more students to put their hands up creates an awkward tension where the teacher will be seen to choose the most worthy student to accept praise for knowing the answer. Instead, lay the ground rule that the only reason for a raised hands is to ask a question, not answer one. Adding wait time is now much easier as the teacher can pause, three. . . two. . . one . . ., before directing their question. Never name a student before asking a question; it gives the rest of the class the signal to switch off because the question is not for them. Your questions can also be facilitated by any of the no hands all-student response techniques on page 31 or 'Questions that FLOW' (page 166), where subsequent questions involve new students who build on the previous answer.

Wait time can also be built into questioning by creating multiple points of access. This includes any strategy that allows students to think, discuss and collaborate before answering, such as 'think, pair, share' (page 128) or any of the strategies found in the Review Wheel (page 180). Any opportunity where students get to review their progress together will result in better answers to follow. These approaches allow students to share knowledge, ideas and opinions, which will subsequently increase confidence and the likelihood of them being able to answer with a correct (or at least informed) answer. 'Making a Statement' (page 166) is another way to create multiple points of access. A simple tweak can turn a statement into a question and this makes it easier for students to tell you what they know – perhaps one reason why they might agree with the statement – rather than what is conclusively the correct answer.

When students feel that they can't give an answer or they provide an incorrect one, it helps to give them a route out or access to support.

In the former situation, you might not want students opting out of answering questions. Therefore, we could give them more time with an instruction such as, 'No problem, Louis, have a think and I'll come back to you in a moment', giving Louis time to flick through his book or ask his neighbour. Another option might be to say something like, 'OK, Louis, tell me something you do know about. . .' This might give the student a chance to give a partial answer that you can build on with the whole class. In a situation where a wrong answer is offered, statements like, 'I can see why you would say that. . .' can be used; wrong answers often come from misconceptions and you now have the opportunity to explore this. In effect, focusing on the reasons and not the fact that the answer was incorrect.

Top ten ways to use data in the classroom

Schools have become data-rich organisations where a wide range of performance indicators can be used to measure and report on progress. Using data in planning, target setting and measuring success is not simply the remit of senior leadership and should be used by all teachers to make informed decisions about learning. While Chapter 6 is dedicated to how we can effectively use formative assessment data to make informed decisions, here we will consider some of the ways that summative and on-entry data can be used to aid planning and meet the needs of pupils in every classroom.

1. Progress flight paths

Much pupil tracking data can be hard to fathom, especially for students and their parents. Visually plotting progress is far more effective and one way to represent progress against a target is through pupil 'flight paths'. A pupil flight path provides a linear path of progression between two stages, usually by Key Stage. A flight path then offers a means for target setting and tracking student progress against their end point. The type of flight path used will depend on the monitoring system adopted by your school. Figures 1.6 and 1.7 provide examples of flights paths that can be used in different contexts. In Figure 1.6, the flight path represents a route that a student might take when they are given a level, such as a National Curriculum level for Key Stage 2 or 3. Over time we would therefore expect pupils to make gradual progress towards their target level. Each path can be projected based on school data or a national target-setting system, such as Fischer Family Trust, MidYIS or CAT4. The only problem with using flight paths with a levelled system is that learning is not linear and students may well deviate from the line. We should expect this and take context into account. Nevertheless, although learning is not linear, it is required and expected.

Figure 1.7 offers a different approach to flight paths, whereby pupils are measured against a 'predicted grade' based on information available to their teachers (test scores, class work, homework, etc.). Here a flight path will be horizontal with a predicted grade recorded and various tracking points throughout the year. Flight paths are a great way to visualise data with students for motivational pep talks, target setting and for discussions at parents' evenings. Flight paths can also be used to trigger interventions where a minimum level of progress has not been achieved.

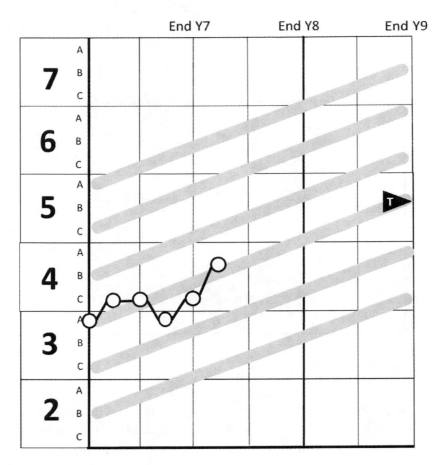

Figure 1.6   Flight path, levelled

2. Baseline sorting

Baseline assessments or on-entry information, such as at the end of a Key Stage level, reading age, CAT4 or MidYIS, are great tools for initial planning. As a starting point, it is a useful exercise to sort a class by this baseline data, as shown in Figure 1.8. Once the data is sorted, we are then able to interact with the information and make informed decisions when planning. In Figure 1.8, the class data have been sorted by MidYIS score and the students split into four groups. Categorising students into four groups is an effective way to start planning differentiation, such as organising seating plans by mixed ability, target grades or SEN. A thank you to Tom Sherrington for this idea.[2]

Although baseline data are useful in making in-class decisions, they should not be used to define your pupils. We should always inform baseline data with

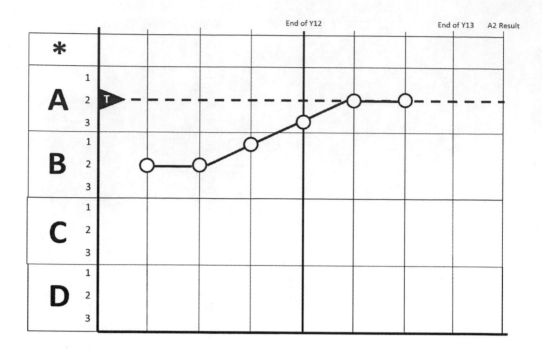

Figure 1.7   Flight path, predicted grade

our own assessments and observations as students progress at their own pace. As in this example, it is sometimes easier to think about our students in terms of groups of learners, whilst we get to know them as *individuals*.

3. Confidence levels

It is always useful to give students a syllabus overview that represents the big picture – everything they need to know or should be able to do by the end of the term, year or course. One way to do this is to give students a list of 'I can. . .' statements broken down by topic area. As the course progresses, ask students to assess themselves against these statements, perhaps with a RAG system. This sort of information will naturally be collected via ongoing formative assessment, but collating your class's confidence levels towards the end of the year can provide a useful guide on planning revision and booster sessions. Collect the information electronically and you can easily graph and assimilate the areas that need the most work. This is also a great tool when redesigning schemes of learning.

4. The exit pass

An exit pass is any strategy that requires students to reflect on or respond to a summary question as they leave the lesson. The teacher can then collect and

Student	Reg Group	SEN Status	Y9 MidYIS
Student A	9W		103
Student B	9Z	E	97
Student C	9Y	N	98
Student D	9Z	P	104
Student E	9Y		107
Student F	9Y		98
Student G	9W		119
Student H	9X		136
Student I	9Y	A	93
Student J	9V		104
Student K	9V		102
Student L	9W	E	117
Student M	9W		112
Student N	9Z		95
Student O	9Y		115
Student P	9Y		117
Student Q	9Z		92
Student R	9Z	P	124
Student S	9X		127
Student T	9Y		90
Student U	9X		112

Student	Reg Group	SEN Status	Y9 MidYIS	Group
Student H	9X		136	A
Student S	9X		127	A
Student R	9Z	P	124	A
Student G	9W		119	A
Student L	9W	E	117	B
Student P	9Y		117	B
Student O	9Y		115	B
Student M	9W		112	B
Student U	9X		112	B
Student E	9Y		107	C
Student D	9Z	P	104	C
Student J	9V		104	C
Student A	9W		103	C
Student K	9V		102	C
Student C	9Y	N	98	C
Student F	9Y		98	C
Student B	9Z	E	97	C
Student N	9Z		95	D
Student I	9Y	A	93	D
Student Q	9Z		92	D
Student T	9Y		90	D

Figure 1.8 Baseline sorting

collate their responses. Using an exit pass provides teachers with useful information that they can use to make informed decisions about their next lesson. For example, a great use of the exit pass is to plan the starter for the following lesson. An exit pass should highlight any misunderstanding, gaps in knowledge or any questions students might still have. At the start of the next lesson, students can be placed in a temporary seating plan based on their responses to the exit pass and required to complete a starter activity suited to their needs.

5. Information-rich seating plan

It is important that we have key data and information on our students to hand whenever we need it, and one way to bring all of this information together in one accessible place is through the seating plan. Often new information comes to us throughout the year about students' health and learning needs and it is important that we can capture this information and put it somewhere where it can inform our planning. On the website, you will find an example of an information-rich seating plan, along with an explanation of how it can be used. The seating plan allows for students and the classroom layout to be edited easily and colour-coordinated for ability, as well as comments to be added on students' learning needs, which appear when the cursor is placed over their name. An electronic seating plan then becomes a living document that can be updated easily and shared with colleagues.

6. Spiky kids

We have already discussed the merits of using baseline data such as average MidYIS[3] scores to group students, but delving deeper into the data to identify students with spiky profiles is another useful exercise. Cognitive ability tests assess key skills such as vocabulary, numerical reasoning and non-verbal skills. Identifying students with significant differences across the skills set can help us plan and design learning activities to meet their needs. Figure 1.9 provides the MidYIS scores of several students. From the MidYIS score in the right-hand column of the table, we can interpret the relative abilities of each student (100 = national average), but a closer look at each category demonstrates that student B and student D are significantly weaker in one of their skills – they have spiky profiles. By identifying spiky profiles, we are able to pick out students who might have a particular area of weakness. Once we have this information, we should provide opportunities for students to exercise these skills and encourage students to challenge themselves in these areas.

Student B – a low non-verbal score might suggest that this student struggles to understand information in diagrammatical forms. As such, they may prefer to see written explanations and explain ideas using words. This student might benefit from practice interpreting data in diagrams, graphs and tabular forms.

	Vocabulary	Numerical	Non-verbal	Skills	MidYIS
Student A	126	122	123	125	**124**
Student B	110	109	**90**	108	**108**
Student C	98	96	98	97	**97**
Student D	**86**	105	107	104	**103**

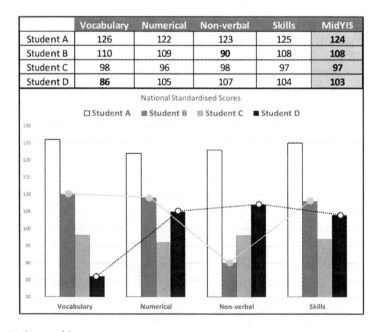

Figure 1.9 Spiky profiles

Student D – an EAL student may well have a low vocabulary score in comparison to others. A student with a low vocabulary score may benefit from word banks and group discussions. Wherever possible, we should also be encouraging these students to broaden their reading in our subjects. In fact, any form of additional reading would be beneficial.

It is easy to make assumptions about students with spiky profiles, but it is always good practice to have an open conversation with them and discuss the types of activities and processes that they find most challenging. In the spirit of a growth mindset, we can encourage them to spend more time practising these skills and choosing paths to help them improve. For example, when selecting the style of homework from a system such as Taking the Credit (page 159), a student should be encouraged to choose activities to help develop their area of weakness.

7. Progress wall charts

It is common to display assessment criteria and level descriptors around our classrooms, but what about targets and progress data? A progress wall chart is a useful technique to engage and motivate students towards achieving their targets.

Figure 1.10 is an outline of what a progress wall might look like. Each column on the chart represents a target grade that is represented by a colour. On the chart, small cards are placed to represent each student. Each card is coloured to correspond to the student's agreed target grade and features a four-digit number. This number replaces the student's name. These numbers are then shared with each student privately so only they know which card is their own. At the start of the year, all students start on the left-hand side of the wall and as the year progresses students will be moved along the wall based on their predicted or working-at grade.

At a glance, the wall chart indicates where each student is in relation to the target. The wall chart will then be updated at relevant points throughout the year, such as a data collection point. This is a useful reminder for students, and teachers, on how each student is progressing. As students reach their targets and new ones are agreed, their card can be updated with a new colour. These wall charts can look impressive and be a useful tool when dealing with large cohorts of students, such as several classes or a year group.

8. Celebrate success

This suggestion is not so much about interpreting and analysing data, but more about knowing the achievements of every student you teach and making the best use of that information. So much can go on in a student's life beyond the few hours you might spend with them each week and it is important that we make use of this information to learn about our students and build good relationships.

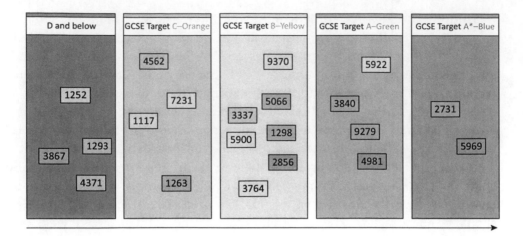

Figure 1.10 Progress wall chart

The idea is simple: know your students and celebrate their success, whether that is in our own subject, in another subject or outside of school.

It is typical that the students who do well in our subjects are the ones who receive most of the praise and recognition. We must always endeavour to praise students for all of their achievements, such as school competitions, sports clubs, hobbies, success in other subjects or even improvement in their school effort ranking. Doing so shows that we care and are interested in the individual and not simply their achievements in our own subject. This information comes to us from many sources: school data collections, school newsletters, staff briefings or a school Management Information System set up to collect and record this information.

9. Effort rankings

Many schools collect and report effort at data collection points alongside student attainment. In such circumstances, students might be given a score, such as 1–4, that corresponds to a description of their effort. Effort scores may also be awarded for various categories, including participation in class, meeting deadlines and listening. Although effort ranking might predominantly be used to report to parents, it can be a useful tool to inform teaching and learning.

An effort grade obviously identifies students who are not showing the desired behaviour for learning and there is often a high correlation with underperformance. In this respect, effort grades tell us little new information but they can be particularly effective when a large cohort, such as a year group, is ranked. By allocating students a position in an effort ranking, we can learn a lot by tracking any changes in position. Sudden drops or rises in position can highlight individual issues or identify students who deserve particular praise (see point 8 above). Any ranking system, of course, has its flaws, as for one student to move up the rankings another must come down. Nevertheless, significant movements do highlight changes in attitude, which can then be explored for students who might need support and intervention. Effort ranking can also be used to inform inter-department comparisons. For example, departments could share ideas for motivating and engaging students who have significantly different effort scores between the two subjects.

For effort ranking to be a useful tool, teachers must be clear on how to award the different scores and use the full range appropriately. It is also important to understand what makes for a significant average score. For example, if a student towards the bottom of the effort ranking has a score of 1.9, is this necessarily bad?

10. Trend spotting

Any data collection period gives us an opportunity to review student data and identify any significant trends or correlations that might inform interventions or influence teaching and learning. Figure 1.11 demonstrates a data sorting form that could be used to collect attainment data for a class or cohort of students. The table compares attainment against targets for certain key groups, including boys/girls, special educational needs and disabilities (SEN), free school meals (FSM), etc.

When students are filtered into the table, we gain a clearer picture of performance and are able to identify any significant patterns of success and underachievement. Although this does not necessarily identify any causes, it does help teachers identify key areas of focus and groups of students to prioritise for intervention. In all cases of data analysis, the numbers are a starting point to work from and to go on to have meaningful conversations about the students behind the numbers. Figure 1.11 demonstrates the breakdown of class attainment – this is followed by some observations and possible areas of intervention.

1. High proportion of boys significantly underachieving. Possibly use more boy-friendly techniques during lessons, such as introducing competitions and instant reward/recognition.

2. Poor-attendance students are falling short of targets – identify opportunities to attend catch-up clinics and small group mentoring on topics missed.

3. Several students have attainment above target – meet with these pupils and discuss increasing targets grades if possible. If A*, identify opportunities for further enrichment.

KS4 Class Analysis

Identify patterns of success and underachievement

Teacher			No. Boys	15
Year/Set			No. Girls	11

Targets	A*–A		A*–C	
	Boys	Girls	Boys	Girls
Aspirational	3	5	15	11
Likely	1	4	13	11

Current Progress	Exam Prediction							
	Boys				Girls			
A*–A	0				3			
A*–C	9				10			
Compared to Likely T	+1		0		−1		−2	
Boys / Girls	1	2	7	6	2	2	5	1
SEN	1						2	
FSM			1		1		1	
EAL			2					
<90% attendance					3		3	

Figure 1.11   Data analysis

Chapter summary

This chapter has outlined a framework that teachers can use to plan effective lessons in an efficient way. It has also looked at a number of approaches in the use of student data and how this too can be used in the planning process to inform our teaching. Strategies for questioning are a prominent feature throughout this book and many of the issues with this most essential and widely used form of teaching have been discussed, leading to a number of suggestions for a good practice approach.

There are many methods of planning a lesson, from the most detailed of lesson plans to a few words jotted down in a teacher's planner. There is no right way, so long as our plans help us prepare and design learning experiences that meet the learning needs of our students. Subsequently, the main purpose of this planning framework is to help teachers ask all the necessary questions when planning lessons, and the following five chapters are filled with a wide range of strategies to provide the answers.

Notes

1 Zoe Elder's excellent blog can be found at www.fullonlearning.com. Zoe tweets @fullonlearning.
2 Tom Sherrington's excellent education blog can be found at www.headguruteacher. com. Tom tweets @headguruteacher.
3 The Centre for Evaluating and Monitoring (CEM) at Durham University provides assessment and monitoring systems such as baseline and curriculum assessments for educational institutions: www.cem.org.

Developing thinking skills

For the purpose of this book, I will refer to thinking skills as the habits and techniques that allow us to carry out a range of mental processes effectively. For example, evaluating, processing information and problem-solving. Under the banner of 'thinking skills', I will also include metacognition – thinking about thinking. There is considerable evidence to support the fact that it is a worthwhile pursuit for all educators to develop effective thinking skills in students. Whether you follow the arguments for twenty-first century skills, check the wish list of desirable skills by the Fortune 500 or cite any of the evidence-based research, effective thinking leads to successful learning. Furthermore, cognitive skills are a key component of independent learning, which a review of the literature claims enhances academic performance, improves motivation and confidence and lays the foundations for children to develop as life-long learners (Meyer *et al.*, 2008). The importance of thinking skills as a requirement for long-term success is supported further by Fisher (2013), who states: 'the perceived need to teach thinking skills has come from a growing awareness that society has changed and skills appropriate a generation ago may no longer prepare students for the world beyond school'.

Regardless of the research, and from my own experience, the need to teach thinking skills seems intuitive and necessary. Ultimately, I want my students

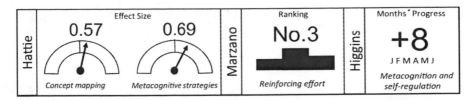

Figure 2.1 The process of 'thinking about thinking' is recognised by much of the evidence-based research for its positive impact on learning and achievement. Furthermore, visual tools to help this process and the ability of students to self-regulate their own learning are also given much credence.

to practise thinking skills because it helps them challenge assumptions, evaluate arguments, appraise inferences, reflect on their learning and progress and, in doing so, develop the skills and dispositions to become effective learners. When good thinking becomes the culture – the way we do things around here – we often find outstanding learning.

In my first teaching post, I remember a staff briefing where the head-teacher asked staff to challenge the culture of low aspirations and underachievement that existed amongst a sizeable group of Year 10 boys. Many of us took to this challenge by reinforcing positive behaviour and celebrating any form of achievement, especially with students from this group. However, an astute colleague recognised the subtle but detrimental gestures of one boy named Cory. Cory was a bright, popular and influential student and a ringleader for this group of boys. Whenever another student would offer an answer in class, Cory would sniff, subtle enough so that the teacher would not hear, in order to show his disapproval. As a group, Cory's teachers and I agreed that whenever Cory sniffed in response to contributions from his friends, and we noticed it, we would follow this up by asking Cory to contribute his own opinion on the subject. Gradually Cory's nasal interruptions were quashed and, although this was not completely the problem, it certainly had an impact. My point is this: it only took a subtle sniff to undermine my efforts to build a conducive environment for learning. Little things matter and we can achieve a positive (or negative) culture in our classrooms and schools by the rules, norms and behaviour we reinforce on a day-to-day basis. Good thinking should be encouraged in all lessons, just as readily as we would expect punctuality and the appropriate behaviour for learning.

This chapter offers a range of simple metacognitive strategies you can use to create a culture of effective thinking in your classroom. They include some simple twists on questioning, some activities you can drop into a lesson and tools to support pedagogy of effective thinking. I will refer to these types of thinking as creative, reflective, higher-order and, to coin Guy Claxton's phrase, 'split-screen thinking' to discuss the skills that are necessary for effective learning.

Creative thinking

In a world that promotes individuality and uniqueness, and where employers place problem-solving near the top of their wish list of desirable employability skills, it is important that we foster creativity amongst our students. The problem with creativity and, well, problem-solving is that we all get stuck in a certain way of thinking that restricts us from finding new ideas and solutions. Here are a few strategies that can be used to help students think a little differently.

Favourite Things

'Brown paper packages tied up with strings, these are a few of my favourite things' . . . Inspired by the Sound of Music, this simple technique will get your students to look at what they are learning in a different way. Simply get students to tell you their favourite thing from a range of potential options and then to justify their choice. Students will find it easy to tell you their favourite band, football team or holiday destination, but what about their favourite punctuation mark, economic theory or element? No doubt, they won't have one because they have not thought about these things in such a way. That's what makes it a great question – it gets students to look at things from a different perspective.

What to do

- Pick a topic in which your students have learnt about a variety of methods or issues and ask them to select their favourite. Perhaps get them to write it down on a whiteboard and reveal it after allowing sufficient thinking time.

- Ask your students to explain their choice with a clear justification.

- Use the responses to lead a class discussion and see who has come up with the most creative reason.

Variations

Once you have asked students to identify their favourite thing, it is a simple step to then ask them their least favourite. Similarly, you might ask students to rank each factor in order of preference and provide clear reasons. You can use this approach to ask even more abstract questions, such as: which historic figure would you have to dinner; or which planet would be your best friend?

Teaching tip

It is best to apply this approach to topics that students will find challenging. For example, students will find it easier to explain their favourite character from a play or their favourite style of art. Instead, choose something that they won't have thought of in that way. If they give you a confused look, then you've probably chosen a good topic on which to ask their favourite.

Consider All Possibilities

As with 'Favourite Things', this technique will encourage your students to think differently. It is a great starter activity to introduce a new topic, or as a tool to recap learning, and works particularly well when exploring cause and consequence. As the name suggests, the purpose of this activity is to encourage your students to consider all of the possibilities. In most cases, we expect students to be able to identify a few main reasons, causes or consequences. For example, in PE this could be the cause of an injury, or in Food Technology the consequences of a high saturated fat diet. Instead of simply asking students to list these causes and consequences, we can pose the question as a scenario. Here is an example I recently used in a Business Studies lesson: *I am a business that is having cash flow problems. Why might this be? Consider all possibilities.*

This question elicited a wider and far better range of answers from my students than if I had simply asked then to list all of the problems with managing cash flow in a business.

What to do

- Come up with a scenario or situation for your chosen topic and pose a *why* question, such as: *I am a tourist town in the South East of England. Visitor numbers have been falling. Why might this be? Consider all possibilities.* Write this down on the teacher's board.

- Ask students to write down their suggestions, directly onto the teacher's board, on mini whiteboards or on post-it notes.

- Discuss each answer with the class and highlight the most interesting and imaginative responses.

Teaching tip

Tell your students that no two answers can be the same. This will add urgency to the task as students rush to get theirs onto the board before someone else. You will also have a wider range and variety of answers to discuss with your class.

The Creativity Wheel

Having taught creative thinking on a number of courses, I have come across a range of techniques to help students think differently. The Creativity Wheel is a collection of my favourite strategies rolled into one model that can be applied to any extended task or project. The Creativity Wheel brings together a number of recognised techniques for developing new ideas and can be used in a number of situations, including developing new designs and products, developing a story or solving problems. At the centre of the wheel is a 'Zwicky Box', named after the astronomer who developed the technique for morphological analysis. Quite simply, the process involves taking an object, problem or issue and breaking it down into its basic components. Alternatives and variations on each component are then listed, rearranged and, perhaps, put together in a different order. Once students have broken down the object, idea or problem, they can then use any of the ten techniques to prompt new ideas. The Creativity Wheel is shown in Figure 2.2 and a brief description of each technique is shown in Table 2.1. The Creativity Wheel, along with a full description of each technique, can be downloaded from the website.

What to do

- Choose a task that requires students to come up with new ideas. This could be developing new designs or products, developing a story or solving a problem.

- Get your students to break the problem or issue down into its basic components using the Zwicky Box technique.

- Use the Creativity Wheel presentation and guidance from the website when using this technique for the first time to help explain each technique to your students. Students then select a technique from the Creativity Wheel and apply it to their situation. Students should complete this process several times using three to four techniques until they have developed a range of ideas.

- Students evaluate their ideas and decide on the actions they will implement.

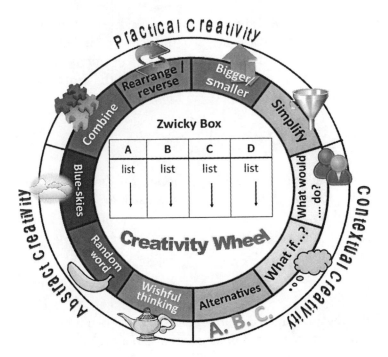

Figure 2.2 The Creativity Wheel

Variations

Instead of offering all ten techniques at once, you could focus on a few that might work best depending on the context. For example, the 'practical creativity' ideas

Table 2.1 A summary of the Creativity Wheel

Technique	Description
Bigger / Smaller	Would bigger be better? Or smaller be more beautiful?
Simplify	Can it be simplified, streamlined or made easier?
What would . . . do?	How would this problem or idea be approached by someone else? How would they do it? What would they say?
What if. . .?	Students use their imagination to change the context or situation in order to trigger new ideas.
Alternatives	What are the options? How could we do this differently? What are the choices?
Wishful thinking	In a perfect world, what would be the answer?
Random word	1. Take a random word or object. 2. Think about its meaning, associations and properties. 3. Apply this to your idea, problem or story.
Blue-skies thinking	A brainstorming exercise where ideas are not grounded by difficulties or what is possible.
Combine	Take one or more features, ideas or factors and combine them.
Rearrange / Reverse	Could swapping things around solve the problem or make it better?

might be more appropriate when innovating new products in Design Technology, so the scope might be narrowed down to these four approaches. A couple of variations could also be used to help students select a technique. For example, putting each technique onto a card or placing a spinner at the centre of the wheel would help students select an approach at random.

Reflective thinking

Being able to reflect on the learning process is an important skill that needs to be fostered in students. Where students are able to reflect, they can self-assess and measure their own progress. Furthermore, reflective thinking is motivational because it allows students to be part of the learning process – learning is not just something that happens to them; they can take responsibility for it.

Plenary Dice

Dice are a great way to add random variety to a lesson. I have seen 'thinking dice' used to good effect to prompt discussion about a topic. The plenary dice works in very much the same way. Each side of the dice features a generic question to prompt reflection and discussion. They are easy to use and can be applied in any context.

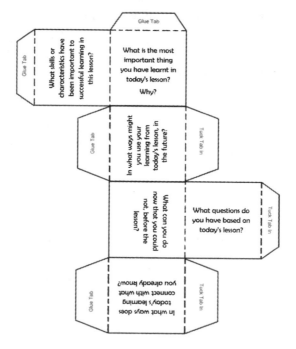

Figure 2.3 Plenary Dice

What to do

- Print out the plenary dice net shown in Figure 2.3 from the website onto card and get your students to make them up.

- For the plenary, students work in pairs and take it in turns to throw the dice two to three times. Students then discuss and answer the questions in their pair before sharing their thoughts with the class.

Exit Signs

Whilst at my first school, I started using a phrase to share the learning objectives with my students. This phrase is 'by the time you walk out that door you will be able to. . .'. It is a simple, yet powerful phrase because it promises a transformation. They will know something, be able to do something or think something that they could not when they entered the lesson. Some of my students mimic me when I say it, but I still like to use it – it's good to have a catchphrase as a teacher. Making students think about their learning and progress before they exit your classroom is very important and we can prompt this self-assessment with signs on the inside of the classroom door.

What to do

- Print the three exit signs shown in Figure 2.4 from the website, or produce your own, and hang them on the inside of your classroom door.

- Use the promise 'by the time you walk out that door. . .' when sharing your learning objectives and outcomes.

- At the end of your lesson, prompt students to reflect on the three signs as they exit the classroom. This process of reflection can be a useful addition to any plenary you adopt.

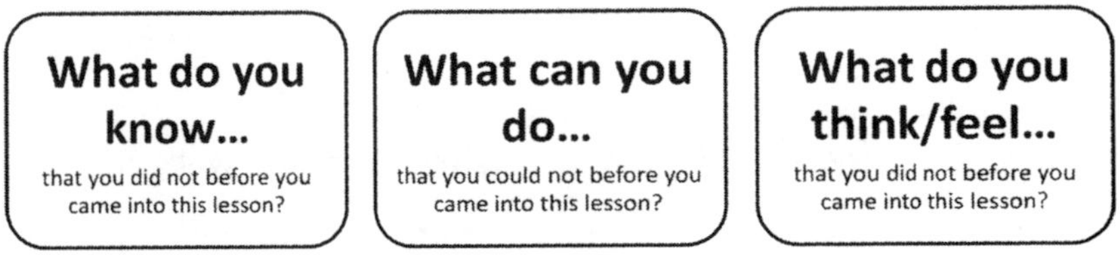

What do you know...
that you did not before you came into this lesson?

What can you do...
that you could not before you came into this lesson?

What do you think/feel...
that you did not before you came into this lesson?

Figure 2.4   Exit Signs

Variations

Other prompts can be used as exit signs to encourage reflection. For example, questions from the Plenary Dice could also be stuck to the inside of your classroom door.

The Socratic Plenary

As teachers we aim to ask effective questions and encourage our students to also ask good questions about the topic being studied and their own learning. By 'good' questions, we mean those that elicit deeper thinking and encourage higher-order thinking processes akin to the higher-order skills of analysis, evaluation and synthesis modelled in Bloom's taxonomy. It was Socrates who developed the art of questioning and he who first professed the importance of questioning as the cornerstone of teaching and learning. The principles behind Socratic questioning are at the heart of most philosophy and critical thinking courses because they give us a structure for probing thinking and learning in the classroom at a deeper level. Integrating Socratic questions in the classroom helps develop active, independent learners. Here are the six steps involved in Socratic questioning:

1. Questions for *clarification*, e.g. 'Why do you say that?', 'Could you explain further?'

2. Questions to challenge *assumptions*, e.g. 'Is this always the case?'

3. Questions to probe *rationale, reasons and evidence*, e.g. 'Can you prove that?', 'Is there reason to doubt this evidence?'

4. Questions to assess alternative *viewpoints and perspectives*, e.g. 'What might . . . say about that?'

5. Questions to test *implications and consequences*, e.g. 'What might happen if. . .?', 'How does . . . affect . . .?'

6. *Question the question*, e.g. 'Why do you think that I asked that question?'

The Socratic Plenary is a simple way to encourage such systematic and deep thinking in the classroom.

What to do

- Download the Socratic Plenary worksheet from the website.
- In the first box, get your students to write down a simple summary of what they have learnt.

The Socratic Plenary	
'*Questions are the only defensible form of teaching.' (Socrates)*	
Summarise what you now know, think or feel based on today's lesson. *What have you learnt?*	
Now, come up with a range of *Socratic questions* that will help you form a deeper understanding of your learning.	
A question for **clarification**:	
A question to probe **reasons and evidence**:	
A question to consider **viewpoints and perspectives**:	
A question to test **implications and consequences**:	
A question about the **question/topic**:	

Figure 2.5   The Socratic Plenary

- Ask students to come up with their own Socratic questions for each of the five prompts (simplified from the six steps above). Alternatively you can complete this in advance using some of the examples on page 52.

- Students then work in pairs or small groups to answer each of their Socratic questions.

Variations

The approach could also be used for as a Socratic Starter, where students assess their prior knowledge and understanding. This would be particularly useful when learning about a topic with which your students are already familiar or about which they have their own opinions. The Socratic approach to questioning is useful for challenging rationale, perspectives and assumptions.

Teaching tip

Although this activity is referred to as a plenary, it is not a quick review and will take time to do properly. It helps to spend a little bit of time explaining who Socrates was and why the Socratic technique is useful. One way to introduce the task is to ask your students to discuss the meaning of the quote at the top of the worksheet.

Higher-order thinking

Benjamin Bloom's Taxonomy of educational objectives and goals has long been a foundation of educational thought about how understanding develops through levels of comprehension and to this day is still the building block for assessment in the UK's examination system. The skills of analysis, synthesis and evaluation require 'high-order thinking' and the following strategies are just a few techniques that can help students develop these skills.

Question Box

Have you ever stopped a discussion with your students because you needed to move on and cover the content you had planned for the lesson? Sometimes the pressures of exam classes mean we just have to cover certain content, or perhaps the questions you are being asked would fit better into a later lesson. Either way, it is a shame when this happens as, at best, it shuns their inquisitiveness and, at worst, disengages them.

What to do

- Use a shoebox or simply an envelope pinned to the wall to create a place where students can post their own questions. Ensure your students write their name on the questions so that you know who to address and which class it is from.

- Regularly check the box and find time in your lessons when it is more appropriate to discuss the questions and answers.

Teaching tip

As an NQT, I was told that it is perfectly acceptable not to know the answer to a student's question, even when that question relates to your area of specialism, so long as you find the answer and get back to them in a future lesson; this shows you care about their questions and are willing to learn too.

Always, Sometimes, Never

One of the most basic forms of question is the true or false question. However, not everything is so clear-cut and often the answer will depend on a number of factors. An alternative approach that will get your students thinking about the hows and whys is to adopt the 'Always, Sometimes, Never' approach.

What to do

- Choose a topic in which the answer might depend on the situation or context.

- Design a range of questions where the answers fall into the three categories of always, never and sometimes. For example:

   o   An acute angle is less than 90º? (always)

   o   The addition of two reflex angles will be below 360º? (never)

   o   The addition of an obtuse angle and an acute angle is greater than 180º? (sometimes)

- These are relatively straightforward questions that can be answered with logical thinking. The best questions will be those that draw out the opinions of your students. For example, 'is it OK for someone to steal?'. Some students may opt for 'never', whilst others might choose 'sometimes'. . . Now you have a debate!

Works well with

- Opinion Line (page 97)

- Four Corners (page 98).

The Question Matrix

As Rudyard Kipling's poem 'Six Honest Serving Men' goes:

I had six honest serving men.

They taught men all I knew;

Their names were Where and What and When

And Why and How and Who.

(1–4)

The Question Matrix (Q-Matrix), developed by Dr Chuck Wiederhold, takes Kipling's six honest serving men and places them in a matrix designed to enable pupils and teachers to ask effective questions. The matrix consists of 36 squares, with each square labelled with a two-word question prompt. Examination of the Q-Matrix reveals how different types of thinking can be generated by different elements of the grid. For example, a 'what is' question will tend to elicit factual, literal or recall answers, whereas a 'how might' question will tend to generate a more open-ended, speculative response. The Q-Matrix is very effective at helping students form their own questions when exploring a stimulus. The question stems selected from the bottom right-hand corner of the matrix are the ones that prompt higher-order thinking.

What to do

- Download the Q-Matrix from the website. Project it onto the teacher's board or provide it to students as a handout as they read or watch stimulus material such as a poem, story, case study or video.

- Instead of setting a range of questions for your students to answer, ask them to use the matrix to come up with their own questions.

- Challenge students to come up with good questions that will challenge them to think beyond the factual information.

- Students then attempt to answer the questions for themselves or take part in an 'Ask The Teacher' activity whereby the class has a window of time to ask the teacher questions .

Variations

Try assigning points to different types of questions based on their difficulty and depth. For example, the questions in the top left of the matrix might be scored as a level 1 answer. Levels can be allocated diagonally from the top left to the bottom right-hand corner of the matrix, with the questions in the bottom right-hand corner being level 5 (a number can be written in the corner of each box to indicate the level). Students are then required to come up with five questions based on their topic. When your class has decided on their questions, they can then swap them with a peer and answer them. They are then awarded points based on the quality of their answers. If students come up with a question from each level, you have a nice scoring system to mark their responses (total 15 points for the five questions). Download an example of a levelled Question Matrix table from the website.

Works well with

- Ask the Teacher (page 135)
- Picture Wall (page 58)
- Special Guest (page 103).

Hexlearning

Hexagonal Learning is similar to mind mapping in that it requires students to take different nuggets of knowledge and explore how they are related to one another. In so doing, students increase their understanding of a topic by teasing out the interrelationships between the concepts within.

In the past I have tried to get my students to make connections between key words and topics written in circles (or nodes) on a concept map. Students are then required to form connections with lines linking the nodes together. However, using hexagonal cards seems not only far simpler, but an intuitive and ingenious step that I must give Damien Clark credit for. Hexagons naturally fit together into a honeycomb pattern and can be linked to a maximum of six other topics. When key words or topics are placed on a number of hexagonal cards, it creates a fantastic visual opportunity for students to explore interrelationships.

What to do

- Hand out a blank set of hexagonal shaped cards or prepare a set with key words relating to a topic, or a number of topics, on them.

- Students work in pairs or small groups to form a honeycomb design of connections with the words and topics on the cards.

- When students have formed their honeycomb, they can then explain why they have made each connection. It is worth paying attention to the point at which three hexagons meet as this opens up an opportunity to explore causality and consequences.

- Once the honeycomb is complete, students can stick the cards down and keep it as a revision activity, similar to a mind map.

Variations

Hexlearning does not need to be an activity that students undertake as a discrete activity during a lesson. The use of hexagonal cards also provides an opportunity for a plenary where students can build a honeycomb of connections over time. Use a presentation tool such as PowerPoint or Prezi (www.prezi.com), or an educational app such as Triptico (www.triptico.co.uk), which allows shapes to be moved around on a screen. Whenever a new concept, key word or topic is covered during your lesson, add a new hexagon to your diagram. At the end of the lesson, get a student to come to the front and rearrange the honeycomb to include the new hexagon. Other members of the class can naturally help them make their choice, but in doing so your students are together discussing interrelationships and, over time, building up a diagram they can use to understand the 'big picture'. This can make an excellent revision resource.

Works well with

- Going SOLO (page 155).

Picture Wall

Like Hexlearning, this is another strategy to get students thinking about interrelationships. The Picture Wall activity also gets students making links with other topics, but perhaps in a more abstract way. The Picture Wall approach is also far simpler than using hexagons and can be dropped into a lesson at any point to test students' relational understanding.

What to do

- Using presentation software, create a wall of 10–15 pictures. Or download an example from the website.

- The purpose of each picture is to have some link to another domain of learning. For example, a picture of a crowd of people could represent society or a tree could represent nature and the environment. Think carefully about the pictures you place on your wall as they will create the opportunities for your students to make their links.

- At the end of a lesson or topic, show the Picture Wall and set your students the challenge of finding as many links as possible.

- When students or small groups have identified the links, ask them to explain their thinking to the class – award points for the quality of an explanation.

- Figure 2.6 explains three of the pictures I recently used in a Business Studies lesson and some of the links that my students made. The lesson was about Marketing.

(child) – marketers will use different forms of marketing to target children. For example, they will put adverts on at different times of the day and use bright colours.

(scales) – there are laws about advertising that businesses cannot break. For example, the Trade Descriptions Act states that they cannot say that their product does something that it does not.

(microchip) – most businesses now use social media to communicate with customers, such as Facebook and Twitter. Direct marketing through text messages is also a cheaper and more direct way to advertise special offers.

Figure 2.6   Picture Wall links

Variations

Another approach to the Picture Wall is to give your students a series of pictures printed onto a piece of A4 paper. Instead of making connections between the topic and each picture, students cut out the pictures and create a chain linking the topic and all of the pictures together – similar to six degrees of separation. Students can compete to see who creates the longest chain with the pictures they have been given.

Works well with

- Odd One Out (page 31).

Connect Four

This activity is similar to Hexlearning in that it encourages students to make 'relational' and 'extended abstract'[1] connections between topics and concepts. However, Connect Four requires students to articulate the connections into a coherent piece of written work, using appropriate connectives to form logical sentences. This task can be personalised to each student, or randomly assigned, and made gradually more challenging through variation. This task works particularly well where the concepts could be the cause or consequence of another.

What to do

- Select between seven and ten words or concepts and display these as a list. These could be from the same topic or a general body of knowledge. Assign each word/concept a number, but do not show them at this point.

- Ask students to select four numbers within the range you have chosen and get them to write these numbers down. This prevents them from swapping words later.

- Reveal the numbers and the corresponding words/concepts to the class. Each student should write down their words/concepts before attempting to construct logical sentences that link them all together.

- When the task is complete, get students to read out their answers and discuss the solutions as a class.

Variations

There are a number of approaches to add variety and challenge to this task:

- Increase the number of words/concepts that each student should select to five, six or seven.

- Group words into sets of four and allow students to attempt them based on their level of difficulty.

- Set the activity up on a 'tic-tac-toe' grid (page 161) and ask students to choose one of more sets of words to link (each row will connect three words/concepts).

- Evolve Connect Four by adding adjectives or adverbs into the mix – for example, four key concepts and four adjectives.

Split-screen thinking

In Chapter 1, we explored the idea that we should not only plan opportunities for students to acquire knowledge, but the opportunities for our students to develop the skills and dispositions to become effective learners. In good lessons, these skills develop naturally through the interactions between students, their teachers and the activities and projects they undertake. As educators, I don't believe we should try to measure skills such as teamwork or communication; to do so is a distraction. However, I do believe we should recognise, highlight and promote these skills whenever possible. If students learn to value these skills and understand how to model positive habits such as resilience, cooperation and hard work, they are more likely to develop and adopt them throughout their school lives and beyond.

The Six Learning Junctions

The popular work of Dweck (2006) and the principles of the fixed mindset vs growth mindset could not be more applicable in an educational setting as a guide to help students develop a positive attitude towards their learning potential.

Believing that your qualities, character and intelligence are carved in stone – the *fixed mindset* – creates an urgency to prove yourself over and over. If you have only a certain amount of intelligence, a certain personality and a certain moral character – well, then you had better prove you have a healthy dose of them. In contrast, the *growth mindset* is based on the belief that your basic qualities are things you can cultivate through your efforts, perseverance and hard work.

Another concept that has risen in prominence is that of 'grit', examined by Duckworth *et al.* (2007), which encompasses concepts such as perseverance, dedication and resilience. Indeed, Duckworth *et al.* discovered that 'in every field, grit may be as essential as talent to high accomplishment' (2007: 1100).

If a 'growth mindset' and 'grit' are so important to success, then how do we, as educators, reinforce these messages on a day-to-day basis? This is where the Learning Junctions come in. After giving it some thought, I decided that there are a number of common situations, in a typical school day, where a student might either revert to a fixed mindset or, as we hope, take the path of the growth mindset. If students can identify these events, or 'junctions', then they can make a conscious decision to adopt the latter. The Six Learning Junctions are typical situations our students face on a day-to-day basis at school and life in general (see Figure 2.7). Here is an overview of the Six Learning Junctions.

Getting stuck

How many times a day do you hear the phrase 'Miss, I'm stuck' or 'Sir, I don't get it'? More often than not, these exclamations of student capitulation also come moments into a task or before it's even possible for them to have read the instructions! 'Getting stuck' is the first learning junction and maybe the most common to crop up on a day-to-day basis. The next time you hear one of these cries for help, smile back at the student and with enthusiasm say, 'That's excellent'. Enjoy the confused look on the student's face before going on to say, 'That means you've got an opportunity to grow'. Overcoming obstacles is the key to learning something new and we should always encourage students to

Getting stuck   The win   The setback

Choosing a challenge   Receiving feedback   Working with others

Figure 2.7   The Six Learning Junctions

see obstacles and problems as an opportunity to stretch their brain. Encourage students to see 'getting stuck' as an opportunity rather than an indicator that they can't do something.

The setback

A setback is an instance where a student underperforms based on their potential or personal goals. Students may see this as a failure; this hurts and has the potential to damage their confidence. It is important that students recognise that they are not their grade. If a student receives a grade D when they were aiming for a C grade, they can do something about it to ensure they get their C next time.

The win

Success is a contentious issue and we should be careful how we deal with it. We all want to be successful; who doesn't? We want to praise success, and quite rightly so. After all, as a teacher we want to foster a culture where success is rewarded. A 'win' might be a situation where a student has successfully completed a task, or received a score or grade that they are satisfied with; perhaps this involves reaching their target grade. In these situations, it is important to praise this success; however, it is also important to ask questions such as, 'Did I do my best?', 'What effort went into my work?', 'Am I challenging myself?', 'Could I do better?' or 'Should my target be raised?'

Choosing a challenge

When given a choice, students, and teachers, will choose the easy option: the task that we know we can complete and succeed at. However, this is not always the option that will help us develop, learn and grow. Activities such as Taking the Credit (page 159) and Targeted Objectives (page 160) give students choice in how they go about their learning and it is important that we encourage students to challenge themselves for the benefits it will bring, even though it might take longer and there is more chance of getting it wrong.

Receiving feedback

With a fixed mindset, unless feedback is unconditional praise, it will be received as criticism. For this reason, students will often ignore feedback because it has the potential to damage their confidence. After all, if you know that you have not done very well on a test, you don't need someone to tell you all about it. At this junction, it is important that students realise the value of feedback. Feedback is guidance on improvement; we must always do what we can to help students see feedback as a positive opportunity to grow.

Working with others

For some students, working with others can be very threatening as this is just another way in which they can be compared and their faults exposed. There are two messages we must convey to our students about working with others. The first is that they only need to outperform themselves. Everyone is on their own learning journey and they only need to focus on their own path. Second, students should take inspiration from one another. If someone does better than them, then this is proof that it is possible and they should take every opportunity to learn from them.

What to do

- Download the Learning Junctions road signs and support material from the website and introduce the concept to your students.

- Displaying the road signs around your classroom can act as a handy prompt and reminder to adopt a positive and resilient attitude whenever students find themselves at a junction.

- Simple reinforcements such as 'What would a student with a growth mindset do right now?' are useful to get students thinking about the choices they need to make in order to keep growing and avoid becoming a 'non-learner'.

The Conditions for Learning Model

As teachers we talk about a language for learning – an agreed set of principles, skills or values that we promote in our classrooms and across the school. Many schools have their own set of values, characteristics or skills they champion and promote through their curriculum that are desirable human traits and necessary competencies for life-long learning. Here is an idea that you can use to agree, share and promote a set of skills and dispositions for effective learning. The Conditions for Learning Model allow teachers and students to build a model of desirable skills that can be used to reinforce attitudes and behaviours in every lesson. The model is built around three components.

- Dispositions – the habits and characteristics shown by successful people;

- Skills – the skills we need to become effective learners;

- Barriers – the internal and external factors that get in the way of learning.

The purpose of this activity is to build and agree a model with your students that everyone can use to enhance their learning.

What to do

- A Conditions for Learning Model can be designed centrally by yourself, within a department or agreed upon as a whole-school model. Alternatively, students can also be involved in the decision-making process.

- If you intend to involve students in forming the model, download the Conditions for Learning Model lesson plan and resources from the website.

- Decide on a set of dispositions, competencies and barriers to populate your diagram and construct your Conditions for Learning Model. Figure 2.8 shows how this might look. In the diagram, the barriers are shown as a wall that can prevent successful learning from taking place. The competencies and dispositions are then shown as the conditions that lead to successful learning.

- Once you have constructed your diagram, it can be displayed in your classroom or around the school, or stuck in student planners to promote the desirable traits and minimise the barriers. The model is therefore a useful tool that students can use to reflect on their learning.

Variations

There is a range of diagrams that can be used to visually represent the Conditions for Learning Model. Other options might include a triangle with 'successful

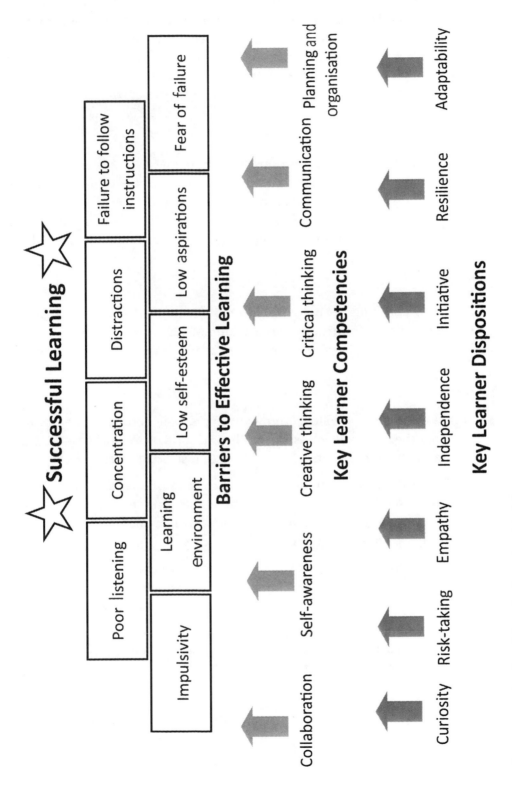

★ **Successful Learning** ★

Barriers to Effective Learning

| Poor listening | Concentration | Distractions | Failure to follow instructions |
| Impulsivity | Learning environment | Low self-esteem | Low aspirations | Fear of failure |

Key Learner Competencies

Self-awareness   Creative thinking   Critical thinking   Communication   Planning and Organisation

Key Learner Dispositions

Collaboration   Curiosity   Risk-taking   Empathy   Independence   Initiative   Resilience   Adaptability

Figure 2.8   The Conditions for Learning Model

learning' at the centre and the three components of the model forming the three points of the triangle, perhaps with the barriers at the top. Another, more aesthetically pleasing design might be to use a Mandala Diagram (page 69). Once again, place 'successful learning' at the centre with the outer three layers being made up of the competencies, dispositions and barriers.

Teaching tip

When creating your own Conditions for Learning Model, it is easy to get over-whelmed with a multitude of abstract nouns. It is sometimes useful to group them together and agree on a word that could summarise a range of ideas. For example, resilience might cover perseverance, determination and spirit. Although each has a slightly different meaning, for the purpose of the task, it will do.

Skills Icons

This is a simple idea to help you promote ideas such as The Six Learning Junctions and The Conditions for Learning Model. It is another way to create split-screen thinking in your lessons with a simple and flexible resource.

What to do

- Place the skills and values you want to promote onto laminated cards and display them in your classroom (Blu-Tack or Velcro works best). Another option is to display your skills as badges instead of words.

- Either at the start of an activity or at the end of a lesson, ask a couple of students to select the skills, dispositions, barriers, etc. that they believe are important/necessary for success, along with an explanation of their choice, opening up an opportunity for class discussion.

- In the former example, this provides the teacher with a prompt to remind students of the attitude and behaviour they should be demonstrating and, in the latter, a chance to reflect on the success or failure of a task.

- Either way, this is a handy tool to use when reviewing your learning objectives and the 'skills for success' you might have highlighted on your lesson plan.

Teaching tip

We often sit back to observe an activity taking place to see if our students are engaged, on task and working collaboratively – sometimes they just aren't. When things are not going as planned, strategies such as the ones mentioned on the last few pages are a useful way to bring the class together for a regroup and pep talk to discuss the attitudes and behaviour you expect.

Thinking Word Cards

This is a simple resource that can be used in a variety of ways to encourage effective conversations around metacognitive skills and thinking processes. Thinking Word Cards are a selection of 40 cards with single verbs linked to key learning and thinking processes, such as contrast, hypothesise, justify and sequence. These cards can be used as a full deck or a relevant selection for a number of effective activities, some of which are described below.

What to do

Download the Thinking Word Cards from the website and use them to encourage split-screen thinking through any of the following questions:

1. How did you go about doing the task? Pick out the cards that show the kind of thinking that you were doing. Can you give an example of when you were doing this kind of thinking?

2. Sequence the cards to show the stages that your thinking went through. What did you do first. . . and then. . .?

3. Try to agree on which was the *most* important skill that you needed to do the task. Rank the skills that you used in order of importance.

4. Select a card that shows the kind of thinking that you found the easiest.

5. Select a card that shows the kind of thinking that you found the hardest. Why did you find it a challenge? What helped you to rise to the challenge?

6. Select a card with a 'thinking word' that was new to you today.

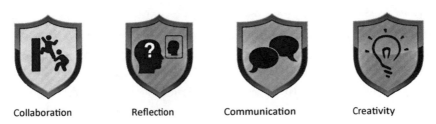

Collaboration   Reflection   Communication   Creativity

Figure 2.9   Skills Icons

7. Where else have you used these skills? Select a card that shows a type of thinking that you have used before in other lessons. Which ones? Can you explain what you were doing?

8. Where else might you be able to use these skills? Select a card that shows a type of thinking that you think might be useful in a different lesson.

Top ten graphic organisers for learning

I am a visual learner and, as such, I like to use pictures and diagrams whenever I can. Graphic organisers are great teaching tools because they allow us to project our understanding and thoughts onto paper (or a screen) in order to demonstrate and discuss ideas and concepts through visual thinking – here are my ten favourites.

1. Mind maps

This list starts with an old favourite – the mind map. When applied properly, Tony Buzan's invention (www.tonybuzan.com) is a great tool for revision and sharing the big picture with students. A mind map is a great way to visually comprehend everything students need to learn and condense it down onto one page. The process of summarising information with key words and pictures is also a valuable exercise in itself.

2. Force-field analysis

A rather fancy name for what is a simple tool to help students make decisions. As such, I also like to call these decision maps. The process of using force-field analysis involves looking at the driving forces and the opposing forces of an issue or a decision; In other words, the pros and cons of taking a particular course of action. In the example illustrated in Figure 2.10 (diagram 2), the issue is placed in the box at the centre of the diagram. Each driving force (reasons for) is then represented by an arrow on the left of the diagram and each opposing force (reasons against) is represented by an arrow on the right. Once each force is in place, students give each a score out of five or ten depending on how significant that force is. Students are then able to discuss each force in terms of importance and the impact it would have on the decision. At the end of this process, the scores for each set of forces are totalled and the two respective scores can then be used to make an informed decision. Force-field analysis is also a useful tool to use when students are evaluating. Being able to provide a balanced viewpoint and identify the most significant factor are both important skills when drawing conclusions.

3. Mandala diagrams

Like mind maps, mandalas are a great tool for taking a topic or whole subject and breaking it down into its subsequent components. At the centre of a mandala, we have a focal point or a point of origin. As we move out from the centre, each layer of the mandala represents a new aspect that can further be broken down into sub-sections. As with tree diagrams, mandalas are great for categorising what we know into manageable chunks. This sorting of information is not only helpful in understanding a subject, but therapeutic too. One effective activity is to give your students a blank mandala that you have prepared with the key words and concepts removed. Along with the blank mandala, provide the key concepts and ask your students to fill it in. This is effective in two ways. First, it reduces the chance of your students drawing the mandala incorrectly and having to start again, and second, it creates a puzzle that students will discuss and plan before they fit everything together.

4. The spectrum

A spectrum is a great tool when dealing with gradations; for example, the level of difficulty, confidence on a topic or the personality traits of characters in a story – good vs. evil – can all be demonstrated along a continuum. A spectrum is also a great way to assess the ideas and opinions of your class. Furthermore, you can turn a spectrum into an active task by getting your students out of their chairs. Draw a spectrum on your board with the two extremes at either end and hand your students a marker so that they can write their initials somewhere along the line. At the end of the activity, you then have a prompt to discuss the varying opinions of your class. Alternatively, take your class out into the corridor and tell your class to imagine a spectrum along the wall (perhaps between two doors) and ask them to position themselves somewhere along the continuum. Once again, you now have an opportunity to quiz your students about their choice.

5. The exploded Venn

Venn diagrams are a great way to get your students comparing and contrasting relationships and characteristics. Comparing multiple factors is an important exam skill in many subjects that we can support visually with the use of Venn diagrams. The only problem with a Venn diagram (multiple overlapping circles) is that they often leave very little space to write down information; quite quickly a Venn diagram can get very squashed when you start to write inside the overlapping segments. Instead, I have found the exploded Venn diagram to be much easier to construct as it allows new information and links to be built up over time (see diagram 5 of Figure 2.10).

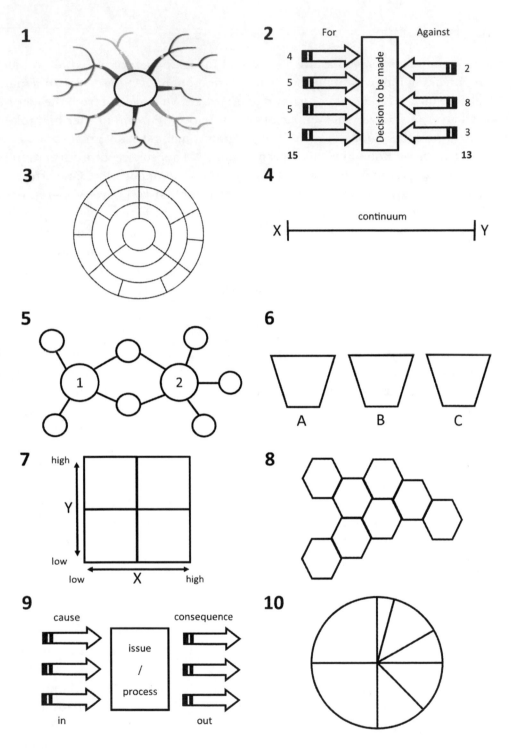

Figure 2.10 Top ten graphic organisers for learning

6. The Three Buckets

The Three Buckets is a simple way of sorting information and ideas and was introduced by Morgan (2004). The Three Buckets offer a simple process of organising ideas, tasks or information into three categories that can then be dealt with accordingly. The concept has a business background, but is also useful in an educational setting. For example, when students are planning their revision the three buckets could be labelled 'nailed it', 'needs review' and 'not a clue'. For sorting tasks such as assignments, homework and controlled assessment, three options could be 'get it done', 'need help' and 'schedule later'. Finally, the process could also be used for sorting creative ideas – 'key feature', 'needs improving' and 'scrap it'. The Three Buckets approach is also a useful tool to use within your departments when reviewing schemes of learning.

7. The matrix

Like the spectrum, the matrix is about positioning. With two axes, the matrix creates a map with four quadrants. When things are positioned and placed into these four quadrants, decisions can then be made about them. An example of this is the market map, where brands can be categorised against two variables, such as cost and quality. Other uses of the matrix could be to plot character dynamics with two variables, such as power/influence and good/evil, or the benefits and reward of different tasks by plotting two variables such as effort and impact. In this matrix, any task that scores high on effort but low on impact is likely to be scrapped, whereas anything in the high impact/low effort quadrant might be done first for a 'quick win'.

8. The honeycomb

As discussed on page 57, hexagonal cards are a great resource for exploring the relationships between different topics. Hand them out as blank cards and get students to write key words on them. When the honeycomb is complete, stick them down and share with the whole class as a great revision aid.

9. The In and Out Box

This is a great diagram for examining any process. It can be used to explore chemical reactions, the cause and effect of historical events or the strategies of two opponents in a game. As with many of the other diagrams, they help students develop important examination skills. The ability to examine cause and consequence is a key skill when explaining and analysing. The In and Out

Box can be used to help students answer a two-part question. First, identify an event, action or issue and get students to write it down in the box at the centre of the diagram. Second, ask students to list all of the causes or reasons as arrows flowing into the box and, finally, ask students to consider the consequences, reactions or outcomes. From this process, students have a structure to build an extended piece of writing.

10. The pie chart

The use of pie charts goes beyond mathematics or displaying the results of a questionnaire. A pie chart can be used to help students proportion information. For example, asking students how much money the government should spend on different aspects of the economy, or getting students to visually represent their perceptions with questions such as 'Draw a pie chart to represent the contents of the human body', or 'Draw a pie chart to represent the weekly spending of a typical household'. Another effective use of a pie chart is to encourage teamwork and collaboration. Before starting any group project, tell your students that you will ask each group to produce a pie chart representing the proportion of work contributed by each member. If students know their contributions are going to be scrutinised, they are more likely to do their fair share.

Chapter summary

In this chapter, we have looked at a range of strategies that help teachers build a culture of effective thinking within their classrooms. These strategies suit all contexts and can work alongside many of the other teaching and learning strategies that are discussed in the following four chapters. Some ideas, such as The Creativity Wheel, give students a process they can follow to trigger new ideas, whilst others, such as the graphic organisers, allow students to visualise thinking processes and communicate them on paper. Effective thinking is often about asking the right sort of questions and we have also explored several strategies that will challenge students and encourage higher-order thinking too. Overall, students must be reflective, creative, analytical and critical if they are to become successful life-long learners and the strategies within this chapter provide a handy set of tools for good-practice thinking in every classroom.

Note

1   See the Structure of Observed Learning Outcomes (SOLO) Taxonomy by Biggs and Collis (1982).

3

Engaging learners

I remember one afternoon lesson just after lunch hearing the '80s rock anthem *You're Simply The Best* by Tina Turner blasting out from a classroom across the hallway. As I leaned back towards my whiteboard, I could see through the glass windows of our two doors the figure of Neil Plant, a colleague and fellow Business Studies teacher, dancing around doing star jumps and wearing a white t-shirt with a reversed baseball cap on his head.

If you are a fan of *The Office*, the UK sitcom that launched Ricky Gervais' acting career, you may also be familiar with the episode where Gervais (David Brent) delivers a motivational management training session to a group of employees. In true Brent style, the training session is awkward, clumsy, cringe-worthy and the observational humour is hilarious. Neil was teaching an A Level Business Studies class about motivational theory in the workplace and had adopted a Brentesque approach to his lesson. Perhaps he could have just played a video clip, but then again, where's the fun in that? His class never forgot that lesson. As teachers we often go to great lengths to entertain and engage our students in the aim of learning – I have sometimes sung to a class, but I draw the line at dancing!

This chapter looks at how we can engage students in learning. Strictly speaking, engagement should not necessarily be the objective of our planning and

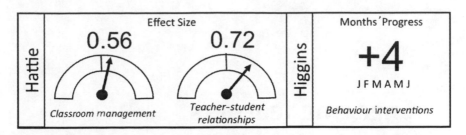

Figure 3.1 Where there is behaviour for learning, there are high levels of student engagement. The evidence-based research suggests that the strategies highlighted above have significant value. Later in this chapter, these are the focus of our discussion.

teaching. Instead, we should see it as the by-product of successful teaching and learning. If we make good plans, encourage students to think critically, take responsibility for their learning, use formative assessment strategies and provide the right balance of challenge and support, then surely students will be engaged. The same argument is true of classroom behaviour – get teaching and learning right and students will reciprocate behaviour appropriate for learning. All of this is true, to an extent, but it is always worthwhile having a few strategies up our sleeve to make the mundane a little more exciting. It is also the reason why the 'Top ten' at the end of this chapter explores some of the key principles behind behaviour management and why much of the research on classroom management strategies is cited in the infographic at the start of this chapter.

Ultimately students are engaged in their learning when one or more of the following factors are present. Let's call these the Rules of Engagement:

1. Questioning – use questioning to trigger insight and make students think.

2. Feedback – show students how they are doing and how they can improve.

3. Working together – as we will explore in Chapter 4, collaboration is key.

4. Active – get them up and out of their seats.

5. Purpose – show them the direction and relevance of the lesson.

6. Compete – turn learning into a game where students can compete against one another.

7. Emotive – connect by evoking feelings on topics and issues.

8. Humour – make them laugh.

9. Real life – make connections with real life so that students can relate.

10. Time limits - maintain pace and energy.

Achieving any number of the conditions outlined above are typically features of an effective lesson where levels of engagement are high. However, the Rules of Engagement must come with a caveat. Trying to make every lesson fun and engaging, apart from being difficult, can, in fact, be counterproductive. The bottom line is that learning and progress is hard work and students should expect this. Similarly, we must also encourage many of the dispositions highlighted in Chapter 2, such as focus, determination and perseverance in all that they do. Engaging learners is not about gimmicks or even about trying to make learning fun. It is about positive associations with learning and building positive relationships between students and teachers, which are the aims of this chapter.

Game theory

In this section, you will find nothing so complicated as real game theory, no mathematical models or an explanation of the Nash Equilibrium; I just thought it made for a good subheading. However, the following games might go down well in your classroom and are worth explaining.

Board of Revision

Whether or not you are a fan of board games, they can be a useful tool to reinforce and recap learning. A subject board game can be used as a revision aid and is also a nice option for a cover lesson. The problem with using board games for teaching and learning is the time and effort required to produce them. Fear not, I have done the hard work for you and produced three templates that can be downloaded from the website and tweaked to suit any subject. The three types of board game include Race to the End (like snakes and ladders), Simulation (like Monopoly or Game of Life) and Board Domination (like Risk). Along with each board come some useful templates for rules, question cards and game features, such as the spinner. Spinners are a useful device to incorporate into a board game because they add an element of chance to the game, meaning the most able student is not necessarily always going to be the winner. The spinner can be printed onto paper and cut out of acrylic (ask a friendly DT teacher) and attached to the board with a split pin. Should you want to design a simulation game that might require students to buy and sell, PDFs of toy money can be found on the Internet so there's no need to raid the Monopoly box at home. Download the resources and have a go yourself or give the templates to your students and see what they come up with.

Teaching tip

Most board games can involve 4–6 players, but should you want to engage the whole class in one game, why not turn the whole classroom into a board. Design your board and then print each square onto coloured A4 paper and then laminate. By spreading the tiles around the room you have created a giant board where each student can stand on the relevant tile as they make their way around the board.

Diamond 9s

This is a game involving two teams where players compete by attempting to talk about a topic, concept or key word for up to one minute (or however long you choose) without pausing, deviating or repeating what they have already said. This is done by working through a diamond of nine key words on nine tiles. The team that talks about the most key words successfully in one minute is the winner. The game can be played by writing key words onto cards or via a PowerPoint presentation, which can be downloaded from the website.

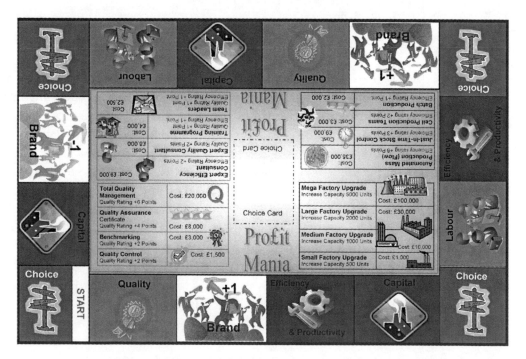

Figure 3.2　Example of a board game template

What to do

- Write nine key terms onto cards or pieces of paper and on the reverse of each card write a number. This number will identify the player who will attempt the one-minute challenge. If using the PowerPoint version, each tile will disappear when clicked to reveal the number of the chosen student.

- Both teams start the game by allocating each member a number.

- Each team then works together to create their own diamond using the nine cards. Instruct each team to put the cards that they are most confident on at the top of their diamond and the ones they are least confident on at the bottom. This is the best part of the game. Allow students at least ten minutes to decide on their diamond because it gives them time to share their ideas and discuss each card. You will find students helping each other out at this point to understand each topic or term.

- When each team has decided on their diamond, call out one number. The corresponding member from each team will attempt to answer a question of your choosing – first to answer wins. This is to decide which team's diamond will be played and who will go first. The winning team can play or pass.

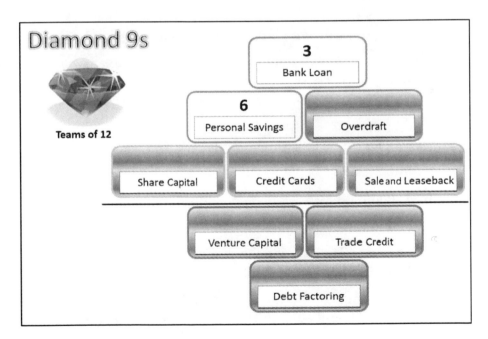

Figure 3.3   Diamond 9s

- Start at the top of the diamond and the number under the first card will identify the first student to attempt the one-minute challenge. If the student is successful, the team will move onto the next card and a new student will attempt the challenge. However, if the student is unsuccessful, the opposing team has the chance to steal when the chance passes to their opposing number from the other team. In effect, the team to complete five key terms first is the winner. The diamond can also be made bigger to include 16 or 25 key terms depending on how long you want the activity to last and how many students you want to involve.

Safe

This is an activity I came up with for a maths lesson, but it can just as easily be applied to any subject. This game requires students to complete a number of problems or questions in order to reveal a combination that will open a safe. Digital safes can be bought from as little as £30 and can be programmed with 4–8 digit combinations. As students complete the activities or questions correctly, they reveal a combination to open the safe and receive a reward from inside.

What to do

- Programme your safe with a combination of 4–8 digits.

- Design a set of questions or activities with a range of answers that match this combination. These do not have to be numerical questions, as values can also be assigned to short-answer multiple-choice questions. For example:

  o Question 1:

  o A. Option A (7)

  o B. Option B (3)

  o C. Option C (1).

  o In this example, if Option B was the correct answer, then the first digit of the code would be 3.

- As students complete the tasks successfully and crack the code, they can come to the front and attempt to enter the correct combination.

- Successful students can then collect a reward from inside the safe (merits, stars, coins or whatever rewards system you have in place. . . chocolate also seems to work!).

Variations

An activity can be expanded by using sums to solve the combination. For example, the following sum requires students to successfully complete activities A through to F: $(A + (B - C) + D + E) \times F$ = combination. The answer to this six-step problem could simply reveal the first digit of the combination. This means your problem can be as complicated or as simple as you like.

Teaching tip

If you don't want to invest £30 in a digital safe, a box with a padlock works just as well. Furthermore, conditional formatting can be used to create a spreadsheet with cells formatted into boxes that turn green when the correct number is entered. Although there isn't the excitement of opening a safe, the effect of cracking a code is still the same. Download an example from the website.

Works well with

- Four-Way Worksheets (page 131)
- Challenge Envelope (page 150).

Wildcard Quizzes

Here is an idea that uses a set of ordinary playing cards to spice up any quiz. A Wildcards Quiz involves conducting a quiz as normal, whereby each student works on their own to score as many points as possible. Each question acts as a new round, at the start of which students are allocated a card from the deck. Each card used in a Wildcards Quiz will influence that student's turn in some way. For example, identifying how many points they will be awarded for a correct answer, pairing them to work with another student or awarding some form of bonus. It is not necessary to use a full deck of cards and here is how the different cards might be used during a quiz:

- *2–10* – points cards: these are the standard cards that determine how many points the student will receive by answering the question correctly. It is important to think carefully about the quantity of each card and the range used in each game. For example, you might want to keep a narrow range of points by excluding the 2s, 3s, 9s and 10s. Before starting the game, it is also necessary to allocate a standard score for a correct answer (I would suggest six points) as special cards, such as the King, still require a point score.

- *King* – free pass: the student can choose one question to play the King card on. They will then automatically get the points, even if their answer is incorrect. The student will simply circle the letter 'K' at the end of their answer to indicate the question on which they intend to play the card. The standard score will be awarded for the question that the King was drawn.

- *Queen* – clue: any student who draws a Queen will be whispered a clue, should they need one, from the teacher for the question on which the card was drawn. Standard score awarded.

- *Jack* – team Jack: any students who draw Jacks from the deck will work together as a team during that round. Jacks must share their answers with each other. Standard score awarded.

- *Ace* – double points: the Ace must select another student in the class, announce it and make a record on their scorecard (it cannot be the student who they are sat next to) For a correct answer on that round, the student will then receive double the points indicated by that student's card (double the standard score if that card is a King, Queen, Jack or Joker).

- *Joker* – steal: the student must select another student in the class and make a record on their scorecard. The Joker will then steal the points from that student for this question, determined by that student's card. They are not able to select the player with the Ace and will receive 0 points if the student they select gets the question wrong. For this reason, the Joker will not announce who they are stealing the points from until everyone has written their answers.

What to do

- Produce a quiz with 10–20 questions and acquire a deck of normal playing cards.

- To play a Wildcards Quiz, it is useful to adopt a scorecard like the one shown provided on the website, as this will help your students keep track of their cards and scores.

- Explain the rules to your class and perhaps include the role of each card on the scorecard or project them onto your whiteboard.

- Carry out the quiz and deal each student a card at the start of each question. As students write down their answers, they should also keep a record of their cards and any decisions they made.

- At the end of the quiz, get students to swap their scorecards and mark as you read out the answers. After the quiz has been marked, students can add up the totals and the winner announced.

- Regularly carrying out a Wildcards Quiz – for example, as an end-of-topic test – will build up a set of scores over time, which can form a leaderboard for your class. As the game involves a significant element of chance, it is not necessarily the case that your most able students will always be at the top!

Teaching tip

It is better to shuffle and deal the cards yourself as allowing students to select their own card can take some time. As students are attempting to answer each question, this is the best time to collect in the cards and give them a shuffle before the next round. It also gives you the chance to circulate the room and ensure no-one is cheating!

Variations

The beauty of this game is that cards can be applied in any combination to meet the needs of your class, and the rules of each card can be adapted to influence the quiz in any way. Table 3.1 shows a suggestion for how the cards can be split for different class sizes.

Table 3.1 Wildcard Quizzes: splitting the cards for different class sizes

Class of 12	Class of 20	Class of 28
1 x King	1 x King	1 x King
1 x Queen	1 x Queen	2 x Queen
2 x Jack	3 x Jack	4 x Jack
1 x 3	1 x 2	2 x 2
1 x 4	2 x 3	2 x 3
1 x 5	2 x 4	2 x 4
1 x 6	2 x 5	2 x 5
1 x 7	2 x 6	3 x 6
1 x 8	1 x 7	2 x 7
1 x Ace	1 x 8	2 x 8
1 x Joker	1 x 9	2 x 9
	1 x 10	2 x 10
	1 x Ace	1 x Ace
	1 x Joker	1 x Joker

Dominoes

Dominoes is a matching activity that is designed to involve the whole class in creating a chain of questions and answers. Each student in your class will receive a card with an answer and a question on it. One student will start the game by reading out their question. Another student will respond with the relevant answer and then proceed to read out their question. As each student is required to respond to a statement given by another student, everyone has to be actively listening for the question that matches their answer.

What to do

- Create a set of domino cards that have an answer on the left and a question on the right. The last card you create will have the question (on the right) to the answer from your first card, therefore creating a loop. Download the example from the website.

- Cut the cards out, shuffle and give one to each student. Choose one student to read out their question. Another student must then read out the correct answer from their card – pause – and then read their own question. This will then continue until the first student completes the answer to the final question.

- This is a nice starter activity to assess prior learning or works just as well as a plenary. Give your class the challenge of completing the loop without any mistakes or pauses.

Variations

Instead of giving each student one card, a set of domino cards can be given to pairs as a useful card sorting activity. Domino cards do not have to be restricted to simple questions and answers, but also work well as a mental arithmetic activity in Maths, as an activity to link causes to effects or for matching pairs together.

Teaching tip

Have another set of uncut cards in front of you so that you can keep track and check any incorrect answers. It also helps if each answer matches only one question to avoid ambiguity and a split in the loop.

Blankety Blank

A set of mini whiteboards and dry wipe marker pens are a must have for any classroom and this is one activity that can make effective use of them. The BBC game show originating in the 1970s is inspiration for this starter activity that is great for checking students' understanding of key terms and vocabulary.

What to do

- Create a range of statements or short sentences and add each to a slide-show. In each sentence, replace a key term with an underscore (the blank).

- Read each statement in turn, replacing the underscore with 'blank'. Each student in the class then has 30 seconds to write down what the missing blank is. At the count of three, all students then hold up their mini white-boards to show you their answers.

- The teacher will then show the class the correct answer on their own mini whiteboard, or use the slideshow to animate the correct phrase or word to replace the blank. Download a template from the website.

Variations

Instead of getting students to identify the missing word or phrase, present a key term and ask your class to come up with a short sentence that applies the key term. This is more challenging and can lead to opportunities for further questioning.

Works well with

- Bowling (page 96)
- Hinge Questions (page 182).

Top Trumps

'Collectible, Competitive, Compulsive'. This playing card game featuring lists of numerical values has been around since 1968 and can be put to good use in the classroom. Creating a deck of subject-related cards on topics such as organisms, historical figures or muscles in the body is a creative way to help students learn. They will become familiar not only with the subject of each card, but also with the relative characteristics highlighted through the categories and values on each card. For example, see Figure 3.4 which highlights some important information on the properties of different materials. Thanks to Steve Bonar for this nice example.

Variations

Even better than making the cards yourself, why not get your students to make the deck and see what categories they come up with? Students can then discuss

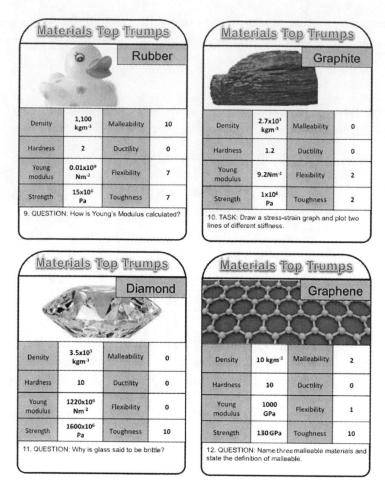

Figure 3.4 Materials Top Trumps cards

the appropriate scores to give each card. This is particularly effective when discussing subjective categories, such as characteristics of historical or fictional characters featured on the cards.

Teaching tip

A nice idea for a reward system might be to distribute a subject-related Top Trumps card to a student for doing a good piece of work. Over time students will build up a collection of cards that they can then use to play the game. Furthermore, playing a game of Top Trumps does not simply have to involve comparing categories on a subject. As in the example in Figure 3.4, each card can include a question at the bottom that students have to answer in addition to choosing the highest score in order to win the card.

Justification Jenga

Jenga, the game where players attempt to remove wooden blocks from a tower without it falling down, can be picked up at most good toy stores and has a multitude of uses in the classroom. The applications are endless but here is one idea of how the little blocks could be used as a game for learning.

What to do

- On each block write down a statement relating to your subject.

- In small groups, students will then play the game of Jenga as normal, but each time they remove a block they must read the statement out loud. The student must then say whether the statement is true or false and justify their reason with an explanation. If they cannot do this or another student can prove them wrong, then they must take another block from the stack.

- As with the traditional game of Jenga, there is no winner, only a loser who knocks the stack over.

Variations

On each block, write down a key term relating to your subject. As students remove the block from the stack, they must attempt to make a connection between the key words and explain it to the other players. If they are unable to do this, they then have to replace the block (not at the top) increasing their chance of knocking the stack over.

Timed Talking

Two popular board games that can be used to develop students' vocabulary and their ability to describe and explain are Articulate and Taboo.

Articulate involves students working in pairs or small groups. One player selects a card with words from several categories. This player is the describer and must attempt to describe the key words to another team member who is the guesser. When the guesser has guessed the person, item, place, etc., the describer picks up a new card and starts again. The purpose of the game is to guess as many cards as possible in the time limit. Taboo operates under similar rules but each card also contains a list of taboo (forbidden) words that the describer is not allowed to use.

The cards for either of these games are easy to make and there is no need to use a board; simply play the game in pairs for fun or set two pairs against each other – the winning pair being the team to guess the most. Allow your students to use the timer on their mobile phones or project a class timer on the teacher's board.

Cluedo

In truth, this game bears little resemblance to the classic murder mystery board game and you won't find Professor Plum or Colonel Mustard either. However, this game can be used to get students analysing various pieces of evidence to draw conclusions to a mystery. The mystery can be set as anything so long as you can create a range of sources (clues) for students to interpret. A clue could be an article, a letter, data such as a graph, or a picture. Ultimately the success of the mystery will depend on the quality of these clues and the trick is ensuring they provide enough useful information, whilst at the same time not giving too much away. A mystery could be linked to any subject – for example, why did the Vikings settle in Britain? Why did the company go into liquidation? What happened on Animal Farm?

What to do

- Create a range of clues for your mystery – between seven and ten might be appropriate. Some of these clues can be red herrings.

- Organise students into groups and ask each group approximately five multiple-choice questions. For every question that a group answers correctly, they are allowed to choose one clue. This will normally mean that each group has different clues and are likely to draw different conclusions.

- Hand out the chosen clues to each team and give them time to analyse each source and form their theories.

- At the end of the activity, ask each group to write down a theory and hand it to the teacher. The teacher will then read each theory aloud before making a judgement on the winning team. Review the significance of each clue, including any that were red herrings.

Variations

Instead of leaving the mystery open for students to interpret, another approach is to present a list of reasons. Each team then has to select the main reason or perhaps a top three. This adds a little more structure to the activity and prevents the teams from going off on a tangent.

Guess Who Quotes

This one is a good activity that helps students identify and learn key features of a topic or the characteristics and personality of a real or fictional character. Students are required to pick out information or quotations from a text that highlight these key features and characteristics, which they will then share as a card game. It works particularly well where students are required to learn about characters so it is particularly effective in English, Drama or History. However, the approach can be used in other subjects, such as Science, in which students can select factual content from a passage in a textbook.

What to do

- In pairs, students are given an envelope and some squares of card.

- Each pair is allocated a character or topic. They are then required to find some key quotations that describe different aspects of that character, but that do not make their identity too obvious. They then write each down onto a separate piece of card.

- When they have selected their quotes and written then down onto the pieces of card, they place these in the envelope and pass it on to another pair.

- Each pair has to identify the character from the quotes they have been given and discuss what each quote suggests about the character. This activity can then easily build into a whole-class discussion.

- By mixing up the quotations and redistributing the cards randomly, a game can be played where pairs are scored on how many correct quotations they identify by linking them to a character. Alternatively, the teacher can prepare a set of cards with quotations for a range of characters, which can then be distributed to the whole class to play the game.

Engaging with texts

Despite the wonders of YouTube and interactive resources, there are times when we just need students to absorb and process a chunk of information from a piece of text. Depending on the age and ability of the class, they sometimes find it hard to access texts, especially if it presents them with new vocabulary. Here are a few ideas to help students engage with extended texts such as articles, stories and textbooks.

Comprehension Cranium

This is a strategy that helps students to understand and engage with an extended piece of text. Comprehension Cranium gets students to use a variety of approaches to process and interpret information, such as using a picture to summarise a paragraph. By using each approach, students are required to explain the text to one another (e.g. explain what the picture is and why they have drawn it). As a result, students are more absorbed in the text, reflect on their understanding and find it easier to recall information.

What to do

- Students start by scanning the text and highlighting any vocabulary they are unfamiliar with. This may then lead to a short Q&A session between you and your class to explain any key words. Students can make notes or assign synonyms to help them understand the vocabulary.

- For each paragraph, students are required to use one of the following Comprehension Cranium techniques to summarise it. Students are allowed to make their own choices, but if the text contains more than five paragraphs, each method has to be used at least once:

  o *Draw it* – draw a picture to summarise the paragraph.

  o *Write it* – write up to five words to summarise the paragraph.

  o *Perform it* – act, impersonate, pose or sing a summary of the paragraph.

  o *Explain it* – prepare a ten-second summary to explain the paragraph. Students are not allowed to read from any notes.

  o *Question it* – come up with a multiple-choice question based on the paragraph that another student will then attempt to answer.

- Give students sufficient time to complete each activity. This will depend on the length of the text.

- Select a range of students to share, perform or explain what they have produced with the rest of the class. Select 2–3 students for each paragraph who have used a different approach – this is a chance to involve every student in your class. At the end of the activity, all students will have a better understanding of the text.

Variations

An alternative approach is to organise Comprehension Cranium as a group activity, whereby each group member is assigned their own paragraph and a method to summarise it.

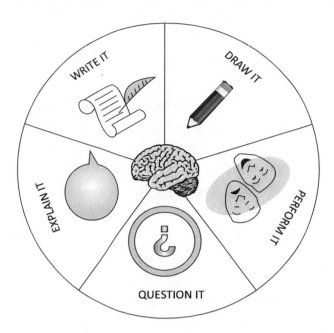

Figure 3.5 Cranium spinner

Other ways to assign each method to a paragraph is to use a spinner (Figure 3.5) or to adopt small cards with each of the five methods written on them. Students can then randomly assign each method by placing a card face down on top of each paragraph. Both of these resources can be downloaded from the website.

Teaching tip

Think carefully about the text you are using. Students will find it easier to draw pictures to represent physical/visual objects (Draw it) or act out a story (Perform it). To make Comprehension Cranium easier, the most appropriate methods can be selected to suit the subject matter.

Text Trivia

As with Comprehension Cranium, the idea behind Text Trivia is to gradually introduce students to a text. Text Trivia involves students racing to find information from a text through a series of simple instructions. By the time you have done a variety of the activities explained below, the students will become familiar with the text; it is no longer 'scary' and they are then more able to look for answers to questions as they absorb the information. At the end of Text Trivia, all students should be able to do a task such as writing a 50-word summary, answering a set of questions or producing a poster based on what they have learnt.

What to do

- It is useful to add line numbers to the text. This will help students find the information as you discuss the text.

- Start by asking students to skim the text – give them 60 seconds.

- Each student should be given a whiteboard and pen so that they can all respond at the end of each round. The following is a suggestion of the types of questions a teacher can ask when using Text Trivia:

  o Write one fact from the text onto your whiteboard.

  o Find a person's name.

  o Find two countries.

  o Find two types of animal.

  o Find the name of a town or village.

  o I will read the text – when I stop, write the next word on your whiteboard.

  o Find two adjectives.

  o Find two verbs.

  o Find a time of day.

- Students will love racing each other to find and highlight the information and, at the end of the activity, they will have read the text several times without realising it.

Dream Pictures

The previous two strategies have required students to read text for themselves before carrying out a number of activities to absorb and learn the information. However, this does not always have to be the case. Dream Pictures requires students to build a picture in their mind as the teacher reads a descriptive passage of text aloud to the whole class. Students then transfer their dream picture to paper before discussing it with their peers. This activity works particularly well when introducing a new topic to the class.

What to do

- Choose a topic that is suitable to represent visually as a picture. Ideally it should involve a range of features or components. For example, deforestation might be a good topic to use in Geography as there is a range of causes that can be represented in a picture.

- Ask your students to close their eyes and rest their heads on the desk. This will help them visualise and build their dream picture as you read them the text.

- Tell your students to visualise a picture that represents what you are about to read them.

- When the text has been read, tell your students to open their eyes and draw their picture. It is important to give students no more than two minutes to draw their pictures.

- After the two minutes is up, students should swap their pictures with the person next to them, who should then attempt to interpret the picture and explain it back to their partner.

- Depending on the quantity of information you give the class, different students will pick up on different issues, or at least represent them differently in their pictures.

- It is not necessary to read all of the information in one go. This activity can be done in stages whereby students build their pictures up over two or three rounds. If you use this approach, it is useful to give students a large piece of paper, or perhaps get them to use a full page in their books.

Ten-word Challenge

This one is a useful strategy to get your students summarising what they have read and evaluating a text. Start by asking your students to read the text. After reading the text, ask them to pick out the ten words that they consider to be the most important. Ten is a nominal number – it is best if you believe the text has more key words than the target you set. For example, if you can pick out 20–25 key words, then you might set the challenge at 15. This means your students have to make a judgement and justify their choice – they are evaluating. Students will need to read the text a second time to highlight all of the words they think are important before they start to make choices. Get your students working in pairs and listen in to the quality of conversations that follow as they deliberate and form their list. Different pairs will naturally make different choices, giving rise to further quality discussion.

Active engagement

In this section, we look at a few strategies that simply get your students up and moving about. It is good practice for students to get up and out of their seats at least once during a lesson and make the most of their learning environment, not least because it adds variety and stops boredom, but also because active learning is fun and increases concentration.

Memory Runs

This is an engaging activity to help students memorise and interpret detailed pictures or complex diagrams – for example, the periodic table, the water cycle or the human skeleton. Students work in small teams and take it in turns to memorise a picture or diagram. They then attempt to recreate what they saw. The winning team is the group that has recreated the most accurate diagram or picture.

What to do

- Stick an A3 copy of the diagram or picture to the wall outside your classroom. If you have a large class, it is useful to place a couple either side of your door.

- Organise your class into groups of 3–4 and get them to allocate numbers.

- To start, all number 1s exit the room to do their Memory Run. This involves looking at the picture for 30–45 seconds to memorise as much as they can. Once their time is up, the Memory Runners re-enter the room and return to their groups.

- Each Memory Runner then attempts to explain what they can remember to the rest of the group, a member of which will start to recreate and, if necessary, label what the Memory Runner can recall. This process continues until each student has been the Memory Runner.

- At the end of the activity, each group's effort is then stuck to the board and the original diagram or picture shown to the whole class. The teacher will then explain the diagram whilst commenting on the efforts of each team. Students are now familiar with the diagram and far more engaged as you explain the concept and decide on the winning team.

Variations

One variation is to change the picture or diagram after each set of students has taken their turn. For example, this might involve introducing the events of a timeline in stages, or gradually revealing different parts of a picture to each set of students. Each group then has the added challenge of trying to piece together the parts of a diagram to construct the whole. In a normal Memory Run, as the game progresses each student's task generally becomes easier as there are fewer elements to recall. Instead, each student now has their own portion of the diagram to remember and share with the rest of their group.

Teaching tip

The more complex the diagram, the better this activity works, as it will be easier to identify the winning team. Furthermore, this is a useful activity to use just before playing your class a short animation or video clip, which explains the concepts in the picture or diagram.

Works well with

- Expert Groups (page 123)
- Dream Pictures (page 90).

Revision Football

Here is an active strategy to liven up your Q&A during a revision session. Revision football involves using a large round ball, typically a football, with key words written on it.

What to do

- Take a large football (the ones with hexagonal patches work best) and write down the key words related to the topic you want students to revise.
- Stand in front of your class and, in turn, throw the ball to the students in your class. This sometimes works best if the class is seated, or perhaps standing if you can organise then into a circle or arc.
- As students catch the ball, they must attempt to explain the key word closest to the thumb on their right hand.
- Continue this process until all students have had a go.

Variations

Get students to throw the ball between themselves and vary the questions. For example, ask students to give a sentence using the key word or ask them to talk for one minute on the topic without pausing, repeating or deviating.

Teaching tip

> Keep the ball slightly deflated – that way any stray throws have less chance of doing damage!

The Writing's on the Window

Here is a simple idea to add a bit of fun to projects and group work. Students love to write their answers and ideas on the teacher's whiteboard, but the problem is that there is typically only one of these in a classroom. So why not let your students use the windows as well?

Using the windows in a classroom as a writing surface is not only fun, and gratifying in a rebellious way, but is an effective use of the learning environment. When students work in small groups to plan, design or solve problems, they will often end up gathered around a sheet of paper. Instead, giving students the option to use the window surface maximises the potential for what is generally an unutilised space in many classrooms. Furthermore, this approach gets students up and active and is a totally 'green' way to work – using no paper or electricity.

What to do

- Buy some glass marker pens – glass markers and liquid chalk pens are fairly inexpensive at around £1–£1.50 each and come in a whole variety of colours.

- Allow your students to use the window space for any open-ended activity such as brainstorming, solving mathematical problems, creating thinking maps, writing poems or designing a new product.

- At the end of the lesson (or day), use a paper towel and warm water to wipe your windows clean to avoid the wrath of the caretaker! Alternatively, leave the work up on the windows for your students to return to in another lesson.

Variations

Instead of letting your students do all of the window writing, why not have a go yourself? Use your windows to set starter activities, extension work or formative assessments. Different activities can be spread across different windows to provide instructions for different groups of learners. Another option is to use your windows as prompts for students to add their own ideas and suggestions. For example, write a concept or piece of vocabulary on each window and get students to move from pane to pane, adding what they know about that topic. Window writing can be incorporated into most teaching and learning strategies.

Catch the Bus

Aptly named for the way it gets students running about the room with an out-stretched arm as if running to catch a bus. This is a team race activity that is a quick way to check prior learning of your class.

What to do

- Create a set of 6–10 question cards. These questions should have relatively straightforward answers. You will require multiple sets of these questions on different coloured cards depending on how many groups you have. Any more than four and this activity gets a bit tricky.

- Mix up each pile of questions, place them on the desk in front of you and ensure each team of students is sat together.

- One person from each group runs to the front of the room to collect the first question. They run back to their group, read out the question and, as a group, decide on the answer. A different student will then run to you and give you the answer.

- If the answer is correct, you take the card and pass them the second question. They run back to the group, and so forth.

- If a student gives a wrong answer, they must return to their group to deliberate the answer until they get it right.

- The winning team is the first to work their way through the deck of questions and be sat back down in their places.

- The great thing about this activity is that the teacher is able to put the questions to one side that any team struggled on. At the end of the activity, you will know exactly which areas need a recap or clarification.

Freeze Frame

This one is traditionally a Drama exercise, but I think it has some useful applications in a range of contexts. Essentially the idea involves individuals or groups of students organising themselves into a freeze frame that portrays a scene or emotion. Give students time to think and then prepare if working in a group before announcing 'freeze frame'. At this point, everyone should be in their pose. Here are a few of its applications.

What to do

- *Mood to Learning* – there are many simple techniques to quickly assess a class's attitude towards their learning, such as 'thumbs up' or using RAG cards to show confidence levels. How about getting students to perform a freeze frame that expresses their feelings about their learning and progress?

- *Favourite Scene* – have groups of students perform a freeze frame for their favourite scene in a play, film or story. As groups do this one at a time, the rest of the class can try to guess what the freeze frame represents. To avoid repetition, you could hand out cue cards so that each group has a different scene to create.

- *Situation Freeze Frame* – the technique could also be used to create a range of situations appropriate to various subjects. For example, the perfect posture for a javelin throw, a scene from a Muslim mosque or a scene from Roman Britain.

- *Peer Modelling* – one way to run any of these activities is to get one student to physically model another student or group of students. They can have lots of fun positioning their limbs, facial expressions and surroundings.

Bowling

This is a simple game in which students compete against each other to try and guess what other students are thinking. One student comes to the front of the classroom. All other students in the class stand up. Those standing have to think of an example of something that the teacher has identified. This has to be something where there are multiple right answers. For example, think of a triangular number, an element from the periodic table, a character from a Shakespearian play or a form of rock. The student at the front of the class then has three attempts to guess what people are thinking. Any student who has thought of the answer announced by the student at the front of the room has to sit down. The purpose is for the student at the front – the bowler – to knock down as many students as possible. Bring another student to the front of the class and repeat the exercise with a different question.

Teaching tip

To avoid cheating, get students to write their ideas on a mini whiteboard and turn it over when their idea has been announced.

Auction House

Auction House is a very energetic activity that involves the teacher orchestrating a live auction from the front of the room. The purpose of the auction is for students to bid on items that they need in order to complete a task. For example, students could be bidding on different 'green' solutions to design a new house, vocabulary or writing techniques to use in a story or skills to apply for a job. If students are paired up for the auction, it gets them discussing the relative merits and value of each item in the auction. The Auction House activity creates a lot of excitement around the classroom as students bid against one another.

What to do

- Identify a range of items that will go into the auction. Project these onto the teacher's board and produce a set of cards that can then be handed to the winning bidders. It is useful to have multiple 'lots' of certain items that might be in popular demand. It is also worth setting a rule that each pair or group has to win at least X amount of items. This encourages them to budget and allocate their resources effectively.

- Allocate each group a fictional amount of money, perhaps £100, to do their bidding. There is no need to use toy money – students can simply mark off their spending as a running total.

- Explain the rules of the auction and how you expect groups to bid. Run the auction, applying your best auction chant, until each item has been sold. It is worth raising the starting bid for the most popular items as this will speed up the process. You can always drop the price if there are no takers.

Teaching tip

If you anticipate that your class will get a little over-excited, one option is to run a silent bid whereby bids can only be placed with a raised hand. Any calling out and the bid is ignored or cancelled. It is also worth setting a ground rule that bids are cancelled if there is any disagreement within a group. This prevents over-zealous students from getting carried away.

Opinion Line

Whenever it is necessary to gain the opinions of students, it is useful to use a human opinion line. If you don't have room within your classroom, take students outside and get them to position themselves between two points on a spectrum – perhaps 'agree' and 'disagree'. Once the line is formed, you have a useful starting point for asking students to explain why they have chosen their position on the line. You can also add facts or information to the discussion to see if any students change their position. For example, is it OK to steal? Is it OK to steal from the very wealthy? What about if the people who steal need what they steal to survive? Another variation on the opinion line is to use the four corners of the classroom whereby each corner represents a different option. Students stand in the corner that corresponds to their choice.

Post-it On

Post-it On is a creative writing activity that draws on the ideas and contributions of a range of students. The activity works really well with extended writing as the exercise can be directed towards analysis or evaluation in order to work on higher-order thinking skills, which is particularly relevant for essay writing.

What to do

- Students sit in groups of six.

- On the board, the teacher writes down six different instructions, prompts or questions. For example:

  o When describing which subjects they like or dislike in French:

    1. Positive opinion phrase

    2. School subject you like

    3. Adjective

    4. Negative opinion phrase

    5. School subject you don't like

    6. Adjective

  o For English/Media, it could be:

    1. Which chapter/scene?

    2. Which characters are involved?

    3. The feelings of the character

    4. What happened?

    5. Analysis of what happened

    6. Evaluation of the chapter/scene

o For Geography, it could be:

1. Cause – human

2. Cause – physical

3. Effect – short term

4. Effect – long term

5. Response – short term

6. Response – long term

- Each student is then given a post-it note.

- The idea is to pass their post-it note around the circle six times until they have got their original note back in their hand with the ideas and answers of everyone else in their group.

- Each student then has to use the information on their post-it note to create the most developed answer they can think of.

Trading Choices

Trading Choices is an active task that involves all students in a mass group decision-making exercise. The activity is particularly good at getting students to discuss the relative merits of different issues and making value judgements. The activity can be run for up to ten minutes whereby students rotate around the class and pair up multiple times to discuss the issue or factor they have been given. At the end of the process, students will have ranked the various issues they were discussing. The activity works particularly well in languages lesson because the activity encourages students to practise their vocabulary. For example, Trading Choices could be used to discuss the best holiday destinations. Basically, the activity is effective in any subject where there is a range of issues that can be discussed and compared.

What to do

- Give each student a card with a different issue or factor on it. In our holiday example above, this might simply be different types of holidays: camping, beach holiday, city break, a cruise, adventure holiday, etc.

- All students stand up and walk around the room to find a partner who they have not worked with recently.

- When students have paired up, they take it in turns to explain the merits of their holiday. Once they have done this, they must attempt to highlight the drawbacks of the other student's card. You should give students no longer than a minute to do this.

- Before the pair split to find new partners, they must decide who has won the encounter and set out the best argument. The winner then makes a mark on the reverse of their card.

- As students rotate around the classroom, they should keep a tally on the reverse of their card of the encounters they have won. At the end of the activity, all students take their seats and the teacher asks the class to reveal the highest scores. All students have been involved in the discussion and the class has ranked a range of issues, factors or methods.

Splat

Enter a range of concepts or key words into a presentation and create duplicate slides. On each slide, move the words into different positions. Bring two students to the front of the class and ask a range of questions about the key terms you have used in the presentation. The two students then compete to see who can 'splat' the words the fastest by hitting the board. As with Auction House, students could keep the words they win to complete an activity.

Making learning real

Students engage with what they are learning for a number of reasons and one of these is if they can relate what they are learning to the world around them. The ideas in this section highlight a few ways that we can make real-world connections through our own subjects.

Ten Minutes of TED

In Chapter 4, we look deeper at a range of websites and digital tools that can enhance the learning experience – one of these is TED (www.ted.com). TED, and its partner site TED-Ed (http://ed.ted.com), is a fantastic source of interesting and inspirational speakers and before long the list of TED talks will hit the 2,000 landmark. Originally started in 1984 as a platform for sharing ideas around technology, entertainment and design, TED talks now cover everything from business, to nature and science, to human behaviour. TED is a fantastic source that we should all be using and encouraging our students to explore. This is an idea to incorporate a bit of TED into the curriculum and get students talking in front of an audience. The task is for students to choose a TED talk, present it to the class and then discuss some of the ideas raised by the speaker in a ten-minute slot. The talks your students choose could be related to a subject or simply something they find that interests them. For this reason, the activity could work just as well in a tutorial or as a form time activity.

What to do

- With plenty of notice, allocate each student in your class a lesson in the future when they will present their TED talk. Decide whether you want these talks to be subject-related or free for the student to choose anything they like.

- The purpose of the exercise is to find a TED talk that they find interesting or inspiring, play it to the class and then talk about it. This might involve giving their own opinion on the topic, explaining why the ideas are relevant, asking questions of the audience or simply explaining why they liked the talk.

- As each student is only allowed ten minutes to show the talk and then give their own contribution, they will have to find talks of a suitable length or select a specific section of a talk to use.

- When you launch the challenge, take a little time to show students the TED website and some of the features they can use to find interesting talks. TED organises the talks into playlists by topic, popularity, length and rating (funny, persuasive, courageous – and so on).

- Start the ball rolling by doing Ten Minutes of TED yourself so that your class understands what you expect of them.

- Even if the talks are not directly linked to your schemes of learning, they should certainly be ten minutes well spent.

Works well with

- Taste for Teaching (page 162).

In the News

This one is surely a staple for anyone who is a Business, Economics, Politics or General Studies teacher, although it has its place in most classrooms. In the News is about encouraging students to engage with current events and apply them to the curriculum. There are many ways to achieve this, but here are a few suggestions.

What to do

- *Homework Challenge* – as a homework activity, each student in the class is challenged to bring in a newspaper article that demonstrates a topic that has recently been covered in the class. The homework could require students to find multiple examples, such as three examples of imperatives used in newspaper headlines for an English lesson.

- *News Board* – have a board in your classroom that you update regularly with recent news and articles. Students are required to read the news board and add post-it notes with their own thoughts, questions or opinions on the article. This makes for an effective extension activity.

- *One to Solve* – this one is a useful way to bring current events into subjects like Mathematics, Technology or Science. Post an issue or problem from a news story and ask your class 'how might we solve this problem with science?' A friend of mine takes his home DIY problems into school for his Maths students to solve!

- *What's It Got to Do With. . .* – project a news story or even just an image and ask students what it's got to do with the subject or topic they have been learning.

- *Tweet It* – use a departmental Twitter account to share interesting stories and subject-related news with your students.

Happy Snappers

This is an opportunity to engage students in your subject outside of lessons. Happy Snappers involves running a photography competition with your students. On a regular basis, perhaps each half term, set students the challenge to submit a picture that they have taken that represents some aspect of the subject or a topic they have recently been studying. Not only does this help students apply your subject outside of lessons, but also encourages abstract and relational thinking. Nowadays, most students carry with them a smartphone with a camera and this makes it easy for them to capture those opportunist shots when they are out and about.

What to do

- Before introducing the competition, take a few pictures of your own that relate to a concept or topic that your students are familiar with. Explain your examples to the rest of the class and include them in a Happy Snappers display for your classroom.

- Schedule the competition however works best for you and your class, but ensure you set a deadline for their first submission. Encourage students to attach up to 50 words to explain their photograph. One way to ensure maximum participation is to set the photography competition as a piece of homework.

- As students submit their photographs, pin them to your Happy Snappers display. In a set lesson, announce the third, second and first place winners and present those students with an appropriate reward. Before announcing the winners, there is also the opportunity to get your class to make the subject links with each picture. Over time this collection of photographs not only creates a great display for our classroom, but also acts as a useful set of teaching resources.

Variations

An alternative to a classroom display is to set up a forum through your school website, or a free third-party provider such as Winksite (www.winksite.com), for your students to submit and comment on each other's pictures. This will make it easier for students to submit their work, share ideas and even vote for the winners.

Works well with

- Picture Wall (page 58)
- Odd One Out (page 31).

Special Guest

Special Guest is a role-play activity that can be used to encourage students to ask effective questions and requires the support of another teacher. Special Guest requires a willing colleague to enter your class for 5–10 minutes and take the role of a character who will answer a set of questions that your students have prepared on a topic relating to that character. This could be a fictional character from a story your class is reading, a famous character from history, someone from another culture or a witness to an event. Consequently, this activity can easily be applied to any English, Drama or Humanities subjects.

What to do

- First, find a colleague who is willing to help. Your colleague will be playing a character, so the more they are willing to take on the role and 'ham it up', the better.

- The purpose of this activity is for your students to gather information, whether that is factual information or the opinions, feelings and beliefs of the character. It is important that your colleague is familiar with this information so that they can deliver it when they are asked the questions.

- Give your colleague time to prepare and, of course, any costume will go down a treat with your audience.

- At the start of the lesson, build up the fact that today is an important lesson and that your class is very lucky because they are going to be visited by a special guest. About ten minutes before your guest arrives, announce who the special guest is and explain that the purpose of their visit is to help the class with any questions they have. Now give your class time to prepare a few questions, but provide them with specific guidelines on what information they need to gather.

- Enter your guest – no doubt your class will know who it really is, but they will enjoy the anticipation of wondering who you have roped in to help with your lesson. Organise the Q&A session until your class has gathered the necessary information. Ensure your students give your special guest a round of applause as they leave.

Teaching tip

This activity works best when your students don't know the special guest. Therefore, a costume that disguises your guest might be appropriate. Alternatively you could involve a colleague who your class is less familiar with. Perhaps ask someone from the school office to help out or involve your older students, such as sixth-formers who study your subject at a higher level. As this activity might rely on a favour from another teacher, you might want to return that favour by offering to be a special guest in one of their lessons.

Now That's What I Call [insert subject]

If you're not so familiar with the pop music compilation series then you could just call this activity Jukebox. The purpose is to play short clips from a variety of songs that relate to a topic or concept in your subject. Students are then required to make links and guess what topic you were thinking of. Students might draw clues from the style of music or the lyrics of the songs. I have seen this activity used effectively in a Drama lesson where different pieces of music were played to represent the personalities of different characters in a story. The good thing about this activity is that you can get students thinking laterally about your subject as they interpret the music and lyrics. This makes for an effective starter to a lesson or an extension to consolidate understanding.

What to do

- Identify a topic or a range of topics or concepts that you have taught.

- Now go through your music library (or record collection if you prefer) and pick out songs that you think have some sort of link, musically or lyrically, to these topics.

- Listen to the songs and pick out 10–30-second clips that work well. If you have video or music editing software, you can make a short audio file to play the clips in one loop. Another option would be to play the songs from a laptop, smartphone or MP3 player.

- Set the challenge and play your students the song clips. Get them to write down their ideas on a mini whiteboard before the whole class reveals their guesses at the same time.

Voiceover

This is an alternative approach to simply playing students a video during part of a lesson and involves students creating their own voiceover for a commentary to support a video clip. Depending on whether you let students prepare beforehand or attempt the voiceover on the spot, it can be an effective way to get students improvising and thinking on their feet.

What to do

- Choose a video on a topic that your students are already familiar with, ideally something that they should be able to explain.

- Play the video the first time around with the sound muted. As students watch the video, they should take notes on what is happening and what the audio might include.

- After the class has watched the clip, select students to come to the front and provide a voiceover for the video as it plays a second time. You can let several students have a go at this before playing the video with the audio tuned on to see how they did.

X Factor Songs

Songs are often the best memory tool for students. So take a well-known song and change the words to help remember an important topic or concept in your subject. Students can also compose their own songs to answer a key question and aim to include key vocabulary on your request. Why not turn it into a competition and have teams compete against one another in an X Factor sing-off? Check out the Geography X Factor songs below. A big thank you to the musically talented Dean Jones for these.

> *I Love You Pine Trees* (to the music of Can't Take My Eyes Off You)
>
> I love you pine trees,
>
> Because you're cone shaped,
>
> To shed the snow off,
>
> And you're so flexible,
>
> To stand high winds,
>
> And you're evergreen. . .
>
> You've got pine needles,
>
> To reduce water loss,
>
> Through transpiration,
>
> Because the rain's low,
>
> Where you choose to grow,
>
> In parts of northern Scotland. . .

Or if Frankie Valli's not your thing, how about a Tony Christie-inspired song about erosion:

> Is this the way to slow erosion?
>
> Using groynes to trap sand in motion,
>
> Re-graded cliffs decked in vegetation,
>
> Drained cliffs are less heavy. . .

Tellin' Stories

The final idea in this section of the book is less about an actual tool or strategy, but more about a general observation. From time to time, we all tell stories to our classes, and by this I mean that we tell our students anecdotes about ourselves, about something we saw on TV or how it used to be in the good old days. Whether or not these anecdotes are premeditated or 'off the cuff', I have always been surprised by how engaged a class can be when they are listening to a teacher tell a story.

One of my colleagues who has always made the most of a good story is my friend Keith Hirst. Whilst teaching together at our previous school and working in the same department, I would often wander into his lesson to pick something up or maybe sit at the back doing a bit of marking. In the years we have worked together, I have overheard him tell anecdotes on all manner of topics, including growing up in Barnsley, football, his three children and his beloved Smiths. These anecdotal stories would often, but not always, lead to a revealing point about the application of economic theory but, the fact of the matter is, his students were always hooked.

As I mentioned at the start of this chapter, engaging learners is about building positive relationships and a good story is a great way to connect with your students. Whether or not we make specific plans to do so, story-telling certainly has a valid and worthwhile role in any classroom.

Top ten principles of effective classroom management

This book is about effective teaching and learning. However, no matter the quality of the mechanisms, pace, pitch and purpose of the activities or the excitement of the content, there is always the need to manage classroom behaviour.

Behaviour management is the main worry for new teachers entering the profession and the badge of honour that some teachers carry should they consider themselves able to command any classroom of hyperactive and disengaged teenagers. Whenever I look back over a behaviour incident that didn't go as planned or didn't turn out the way I had hoped, there's normally something I could have done better, said in a different way or tackled in a different manner. No matter what stage of our career we are at or our level of confidence in dealing with behaviour issues, it is always worthwhile reflecting on a few principles for effective practice in classroom management. As before, we will explore behaviour management strategies through a 'top ten' of principles that will stand any teacher in good stead.

To outline these ten principles, we will consider how they might be played out during a typical lesson.

INCIDENT

Students start to arrive at the lesson, where they are met with a set of instructions for a starter activity on the board.	All students have arrived in the lesson and settled to work. Students are working on the starter activity and quietly making notes on their mini whiteboards. Two or three students are still chatting and have not got their equipment out.	Nearly all students have completed the starter activity and are ready to review their ideas and introduce the lesson objectives and intended outcomes.	Following the starter activity and review, you are explaining the first activity where students will work in pairs to plan a piece of work. Out of the corner of your eye, you can see Sophie and Halima in the corner quietly chatting and not listening to your instructions.	By the hour, the class have rearranged themselves into small teams and are working on a group exercise. Kieran is sat leaning back on his chair with his feet on the table.

STRATEGY

1. Meet and greet	2. Assume conformity	3. Instructional cues	4. Pause and proximity	5. Positive instruction
1. Meet and greet – Greet students as they enter your classroom and meet them with a smile. This will always get the lesson off on a positive note and give you the opportunity to issue a set of instructions and deal with any issues before students step foot inside your classroom. For example, resolving any issues with uniform or calming down a student who is upset or overexcited about something that has taken place at lunchtime. The classroom is a learning environment and every student who steps across the threshold must be ready to learn. Meeting and greeting is your way to check this in a positive way. If you are unable to arrive at the lesson before your students, set some procedures that all students should follow as they arrive to help them get settled whilst you check that everyone is ready.	**2. Assume conformity –** Move towards the students and remind them that they have three minutes left to complete the starter activity (with a friendly manner), then move away to support and check the progress of other students. Presuming conformity shows that we fully expect students to follow our instructions. As such, we don't need to stand over a student until they conform. Although this is a trivial incident and the students will no doubt have got themselves on task by the time you return, waiting for students to conform lays down a challenge, which can be aggressive. Moving away or focusing your attention on something else gives students time to respond positively.	**3. Instructional cues –** In order to ensure my students are ready to carry on, I will always use a simple method of counting down from 3 to 1. After each count, I tell my students what I am expecting to see – for example, '3. People should be putting their pens down; 2. Eyes on me; 1. Just waiting for two more'. Simple instructional cues help build routines and reinforce positive behaviour. As highlighted above, it is a useful exercise to state the obvious to your class, explaining what you are doing ('I'm just coming round to check on progress'), what they should be doing ('At this point I would expect most of you to be. . .') and what you are able to observe ('I can see that most people are on task now'). Yet another subtle cue to improve focus and concentration is lowering of your voice. If students have to strain to hear you, it's harder for them to get involved in other distractions.	**4. Pause and proximity –** These are two of the best non-verbal strategies for dealing with low-level disruption. Students may try to quietly talk under you as you address the class and may continue to do this whilst you are in full flow if unchecked. A strategic pause will normally grab their attention and show that you are unwilling to continue without everyone listening. Moving around the room and reducing the proximity between you and any low-level disruption will generally have the same effect. In a noisy classroom, waiting for students to pay attention is just as important; never compromise on their attention. However, it will normally take them longer to comply. No matter how long it takes, wait. . . and then reinforce your rules and expectations. Your patience will pay dividends in the long run.	**5. Positive instruction –** Instead of chastising the student by telling them to 'get their feet down', it is better to use positive instructions, such as 'sit up straight and make a start, Kieran. . . thank you'. Positive instructions are far better at evoking positive reactions and demonstrate exactly what you are looking for. Notice how this instruction does not use the word 'please'; neither did I use the phrase 'can you'. Instead, consent was assumed and students should always be thanked for this.

...dents have been ...n a random number ...told to create new ...ups where they will ...re their ideas with ...ers. The class get ...o move to their ...seats, but Kieran ...tests because he ...sn't want to work ...anyone else.	All groups have now formed but you have one grumpy student who still has not conformed.	Kieran decides to join the new group, but throws his bag down in the corner of the room and slams down onto his seat with a grunt.	The final activity has finished and you are collecting feedback from each group. As before, Halima doesn't seem to be concentrating. You use pause and proximity and then stop the feedback session to remind Halima of the class rules. She protests and says that other people have been talking too.	Following the plenary, students stand behind their chairs and you dismiss the class. There is a lesson straight after this one so you ask Kieran to come and see you the next morning.

...onsistency – All ...ools should have ...lear classroom ...haviour policy. This is ...re to protect students ...d provide consistent ...delines for what ...xpected from you ...d the school. At this ...nt, it might be worth ... minding Kieran of the ...es and how they apply ...all students. Making ...e your classroom ...es are simple, ...nsistent and show a ...ar route of escalation ...he best way to ...ply a consistent ...proach. As before, ...ow this reminder ...repeating your ...truction and assume ...nformity.	**7. Choice** – It would now seem like the right time to impose an ultimatum on this student. They have been reminded of your expectations and given a chance to comply. At this point the best thing to do is deliver 'the choice'. 'Alright Kieran, you know the school rules. If you insist on not participating you will be choosing to go to the sanctions room. I'll give you one minute to make up your mind.' The fact that this is a choice that the student has to make clearly puts the responsibility in the student's hands. You won't be sending Kieran to the sanctions room; he will be opting to go there based on a clear set of rules. It is also worth mentioning that any escalation of classroom sanctions, such as moving seats, detentions, phone calls home, should always be reversible. Students must be able to redeem themselves by demonstrating positive behaviour for learning. Otherwise, with no 'way out', we can only expect more of the same behaviour that got the student into trouble in the first place. Obviously there are exceptions to this rule, but having a de-escalation of sanctions allows the teacher to focus on the positives.	**8. Ignore secondary behaviour** – Kieran has followed your instructions and joined his new group. It seems that Kieran is unlikely to be a particularly enthused participant in his group, but for now we will ignore his negative behaviour and focus on the fact that he has complied with your instructions. Ignoring secondary behaviour might be necessary at this point as confronting it right now is likely to escalate the problem and lead to confrontation. You just want to focus on the progress of the rest of the class; you can deal with Kieran later.	**9. Partial agreement** – Students have excellent radar for fairness and they will sniff out any perceived injustice if they are on the receiving end. Your response to Halima could be: 'Perhaps, but I still need you to be 100 per cent focused on the lesson.' You have not disagreed with Halima or engaged in her counterargument. You could also follow this up by reminding Halima of her 'choice'. Students will always protest their innocence or claim that someone else was doing it too. As teachers we can't see everything, we can only deal with the issues we see in a consistent and fair way without favouritism or prejudice. It might be worth making this point clear to your students too.	**10. Repair and rebuild** – On your own terms and without an audience, you speak with Kieran to discuss his behaviour during your lesson the previous day. You first explain why it is important for students to be able to work with different people and that his behaviour was unacceptable. At this point, you might choose to bring up Kieran's secondary behaviour and that this alone justified a sanction – you won't let it go unchecked a second time.

Give Kieran the opportunity to explain his behaviour. There may be an underlying reason that you should know about or can help Kieran with. Ultimately, you want Kieran to appreciate why he was in the wrong and what you expect of him in the future. Taking the time to repair and rebuild is very important. It allows you to clear the air and resolve any issues that you might not have been able to address during the lesson. Above all, repairing and rebuilding is about ensuring students understand that any conflicts are not personal and the focus during lessons should always be about learning. |

These ten principles offer teachers a few guiding principles to help manage a safe learning environment where every student is able to make progress. The key to any approach to classroom management is that it is built on a clear and simple set of rules with procedures for escalating issues. It is sometimes useful to think of our approach to classroom management as a four-step process, which is outlined in Figure 3.6. At the bottom of the pyramid, we have the proactive principles. These are the strategies that we might use before any behavioural issues arise. In the second and third tiers are the reactive principles that we might use to manage attention, attitudes and behaviour. At the fourth tier, it is necessary for us to enforce the rules and procedures that are typically laid out in our school's behaviour policy. Of course, at tier two and tier three we will have already reminded students of our expectations and given out a warning. As discussed in our timeline of events, the final stage is to, whenever possible, repair and rebuild relationships by confirming your expectations and ensuring the focus is on learning.

Chapter summary

In this chapter, we have looked at a range of strategies that can help engage students in learning. These strategies allow us to recap and reinforce knowledge,

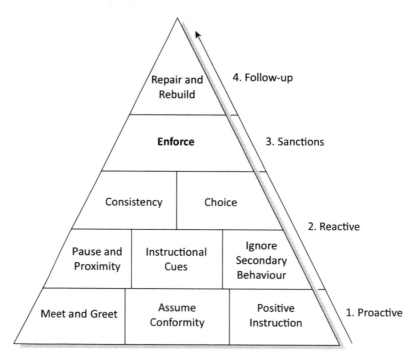

Figure 3.6   The Classroom Management Pyramid

test understanding, practise skills, check progress and, from time to time, add a bit of a zing to the lesson. However, alone these ideas are just gimmicks if they are not built into well-planned lessons where students are challenged to think and appreciate the relevance of what they are learning. These ideas are all useful strategies to have in our arsenal as teachers and are most effective when used in measure. Furthermore, the principles of classroom management discussed in this chapter work best when part of established routines and procedures that are consistently applied day in, day out. These strategies count for naught if we don't know our students and show an interest in who they are. They need to know that we care and that everything that goes on in the classroom is about them. When we show them this, we are able to build positive relationships and the behaviour for learning usually follows.

4

Collaborative learning

Picture an outstanding lesson and what do you see? What's going on in the lesson? What is the teacher doing? What are the students up to? For some, the image conjured might be a calm classroom where students sit studiously with their heads in a book, but I would guess that most of us have pictured a classroom where students are working together. They are engaged in dialogue with the teacher and their peers, sharing ideas and opinions, asking questions and working on tasks and problems together. Whenever I have worked with groups of teachers to discuss and draw out the key features of outstanding learning, a common factor that always prevails is some level of cooperation and collaboration between students. Sometimes you can walk into a lesson and instantly know it is outstanding because the learning is so palpable. There is a certain buzz to a lesson where students are working purposefully together in small groups. Indeed, it is harder not to find good examples of learning when these conditions are present. Evidence of learning is much harder to find in quiet lessons where students work in isolation.

Collaborative approaches to learning dominate the evidence-based research for the impact they have on student achievement. When compared to more traditional methods where students passively receive information from a

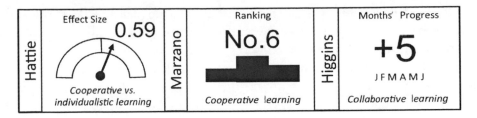

Figure 4.1 The evidence-based research makes a strong case for the importance of learning together.

teacher, cooperative, problem-based learning has been shown to improve student engagement and retention of classroom material (Prince, 2004). Furthermore, more than 1,200 studies comparing cooperative, competitive and individualistic efforts have found that cooperative learning methods improve students' time on tasks and intrinsic motivation to learn (Johnson & Johnson, 2009). This is unsurprising if we consider learning as a social process. Abraham Maslow's popular theory of human motivation represented through his Hierarchy of Needs (1943) identifies five distinct levels of human motivation, which are outlined in Figure 4.2. Although the hierarchical nature of human needs and motivations has been criticised, the pyramid has become the de facto way to present Maslow's theory. Here I have suggested how the five basic human needs might be fulfilled in a classroom context, from the basic needs through to self-actualisation – the desire to become everything that one is capable of becoming. A few slight tweaks might be necessary should we examine the concept from a whole-school perspective, but Figure 4.2 provides a suggestion on how, as teachers, we might help our

Figure 4.2 Maslow in the classroom

students achieve these 'needs' in our lessons. To me, it seems fairly obvious that their love and belonging needs would come from opportunities to collaborate with others and feel part of a learning community.

Collaborative learning works best when deployed for enquiry, idea generation and problem-solving. Real-world problems are solved by small groups of people working in this way and if we are to prepare our students for their life ahead, then this is yet another reason to learn collaboratively. Have a look at Figure 4.3 and complete the following exercise.

Figure 4.3 presents a spectrum between two styles of learning. On the left is teaching and learning designed to acquire knowledge. On the right is teaching and learning centred around enquiry and problem-solving. Where would you place your own teaching on this spectrum?

Of course, there is no right answer and it could be argued that students are unable to solve problems without first acquiring the relevant knowledge, but your decision may give some indication to the style you adopt as a teacher. In classrooms where the purpose is for students to acquire new knowledge, we typically see students being taught a subject. Whereas, at the opposite end of the spectrum, we see students making sense of a subject.

Through ICT and the popularity of the 'flipped classroom',[1] it is far easier for students to acquire knowledge through a website or the thousands of YouTube channels dedicated to learning. Furthermore, digital tools have made it much easier for teachers to share information and for students to collaborate beyond the confines of the classroom. Teachers who make use of the 'flipped' approach to learning naturally move their lessons towards the right of the spectrum where the teacher adopts the role of a facilitator instead of an expert. ICT plays into the hands of collaborative learning and this is why this book explores some of the best digital tools currently available to teachers as a 'top ten' at the end of this chapter.

Despite extensive evidence that collaborative approaches to learning are beneficial at all levels, it is not so easy to accomplish and requires far more thought and planning than simply putting students into groups with a task to complete.

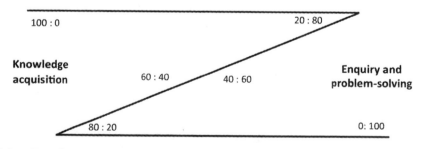

Figure 4.3   Teaching spectrum

In fact, getting students to work in small groups, whether designed by the teacher or left for the pupils to form, can have a detrimental effect on learning.

There have been times when I have asked my students to get into small groups and immediately regretted it. There is no telling what will ensue when you give this instruction. Often groups will form naturally and without fuss, but at times I have observed a social meltdown as students test their allegiances and fight for membership to a friendship group where they want to belong. There is nothing more upsetting than seeing students left out or excluded by their peers and we must always avoid these situations whenever possible. Even when groups are formed successfully, there is no guarantee that they will function as we hoped. There is nothing more frustrating than the 'free rider', who takes collaboration as an opportunity to let others do the work for them, or the group that fractures and splits because its members couldn't agree on what to do.

For collaborative activities to work, students must develop many of the skills and dispositions discussed in Chapter 2. Whenever students work together in small groups, they must see it as an opportunity to develop their communication, teamwork and leadership skills and to test their ability to listen, be patient and compromise. Raising the profile of these virtues, amongst others, is just as important as the problems and tasks we ask our students to solve. Students must also take part in activities that are effectively designed to encourage cooperation and collaboration. In classrooms where learners collaborate effectively, three characteristics can often be observed:

1. *Positive interdependence* – activities are designed so that students can only succeed when the group as a whole succeeds. Often this will be achieved when each student has a unique role and contribution to make that others rely on.

2. *Accountability* – learners recognise that they have an identity as a group. They know they will be held accountable as part of that group and for their own contribution to that group.

3. *Community* – students see themselves as learners within a learning community that they contribute towards and benefit from. Learning in different groups with people from outside their direct friendship group is the norm and happens on a regular basis.

The strategies in this chapter have been selected for their effectiveness in helping teachers to organise the collaborative structures in their classroom and to achieve the three characteristics outlined above.

Fostering shared ownership of learning

Learning Leaders

A while back, I observed a Year 5 Maths lesson. I got there earlier than the teacher or the students so sat myself down in the corner. It was break time and a few minutes before the bell rang a handful of children started to filter in. A few gave me a curious glance, but on the whole I was shown little consideration, as the students got on with what seemed to be routine tasks. One girl collected a set of whiteboards and started handing them out like place mats, another boy went straight to the teacher's whiteboard and began to wipe off the scrawl from the previous lesson and a third was making light work of rearranging chairs into an arc at the front of the room.

During my observation, it was clear that most students had some form of role, even if that role simply involved counting the scissors back in at the end of the lesson. Apart from being impressed with the division of labour orchestrated by this Year 5 primary school teacher, I was also particularly fascinated by how much the students owned their learning space and the sense of teamwork shared between the students and their teacher. The learning was purposeful, collaborative and, above all, student-led.

From KS3, students rarely have the privilege of owning a learning environment for any length of time beyond a single lesson, and perhaps they lose some of these independent qualities that they nurture so well at primary school. Here is one approach I have recently used to hand responsibility back to my classes, save me a bit of time and legwork and, above all, create a sense of teamwork and unity within my lessons. I am quite a forgetful person, so handing the responsibility of these important tasks over to my students, as to not forget, has been an added boon.

Learning Leaders are 12 student roles that a teacher can adopt within their classroom. Each role has a particular focus and contribution to the learning of the whole class. The Learning Leader cards (some of which are shown in Figure 4.4) can be handed out at the start of a lesson, either when greeting students at the classroom door or when allocating them to a seating plan, and provide students with instructions on how to fulfil that role. It makes sense to rotate these roles each lesson to ensure all students get the chance to be a Learning Leader and experience different responsibilities.

The following few pages give a description of each Learning Leader and next to each a suggestion on when that role might become active during a lesson. You could introduce Learning Leaders gradually over time or pick out particular roles to suit the lesson you are teaching. These are just some of the roles that have worked for me, but why not have a go at coming up with some of your own?

Dictionary Dude (active – throughout the lesson)

Quite simply, the Dictionary Dude is the student who checks spellings for other students or the whole class. Teachers often write spellings on the board, but this could be left to the Dictionary Dude, or perhaps the student who the Dictionary Dude looks up the spelling for. Therefore, getting double practice at the spelling and sharing it with the rest of the class.

A second role of the Dictionary Dude is to look up any words that a student might be unfamiliar with. The Dictionary Dude can then come to the front and write the definition on the board. It might also be useful to double-up this role with a second student, a Dictionary Deputy if you like, who can be responsible for finding synonyms from a thesaurus – a key role in any descriptive or creative writing task.

Objectives Overseer (active – throughout a lesson but particularly at the start and end)

The Objectives Overseer has several tasks to carry out. The first comes at the start of the lesson and is to make sure everyone is aware of the lesson objectives. This might involve asking the teacher to clarify them if they have not been made explicit. As the lesson progresses, the role of the Objectives Overseer is then to monitor progress and, where necessary, highlight when they believe an objective, or part of an objective, has been met. In doing so, the Objective Overseer is highlighting the class's progress. To do this, the Objectives Overseer might hold up their Learning Leader card to attract the teacher's attention. For example, the Objectives Overseer could be encouraged to make statements like 'Sir, I think we've met the first objective today because. . .'.

Where this approach is not appropriate to the style and purpose of the lesson, the Objectives Overseer will contribute their ideas at the end of the lesson and provide their opinion on whether they believe they have met the lesson objectives. This can then be followed up with the teacher asking, 'Can you explain why?' or 'How do you know?' As the rest of the class listens in, they will also reflect on their own progress. This phase of questioning works well just before or after a plenary activity.

Time Technician (active – as necessary)

The Time Technician is a very practical role that keeps the rest of the students focused and on task. The Time Technician acts as a timekeeper and supports the teacher when they set a timed activity. The Time Technician is given freedom to remind the class of how long they have left on a specific task or element of the lesson. It helps if the Time Technician has a wristwatch, is provided with a stopwatch or is able to use either of these on their mobile phone.

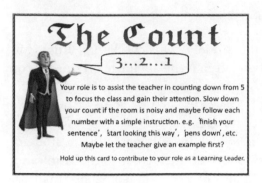

The Count
3...2...1

Your role is to assist the teacher in counting down from 5 to focus the class and gain their attention. Slow down your count if the room is noisy and maybe follow each number with a simple instruction. e.g. 'finish your sentence', 'start looking this way', 'pens down', etc. Maybe let the teacher give an example first?

Hold up this card to contribute to your role as a Learning Leader.

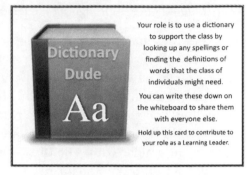

Dictionary Dude
Aa

Your role is to use a dictionary to support the class by looking up any spellings or finding the definitions of words that the class of individuals might need.

You can write these down on the whiteboard to share them with everyone else.

Hold up this card to contribute to your role as a Learning Leader.

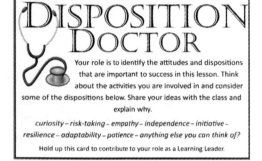

DISPOSITION DOCTOR

Your role is to identify the attitudes and dispositions that are important to success in this lesson. Think about the activities you are involved in and consider some of the dispositions below. Share your ideas with the class and explain why.

curiosity – risk-taking – empathy – independence – initiative – resilience – adaptability – patience – anything else you can think of?

Hold up this card to contribute to your role as a Learning Leader.

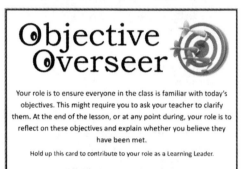

Objective Overseer

Your role is to ensure everyone in the class is familiar with today's objectives. This might require you to ask your teacher to clarify them. At the end of the lesson, or at any point during, your role is to reflect on these objectives and explain whether you believe they have been met.

Hold up this card to contribute to your role as a Learning Leader.

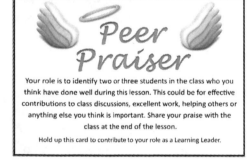

Peer Praiser

Your role is to identify two or three students in the class who you think have done well during this lesson. This could be for effective contributions to class discussions, excellent work, helping others or anything else you think is important. Share your praise with the class at the end of the lesson.

Hold up this card to contribute to your role as a Learning Leader.

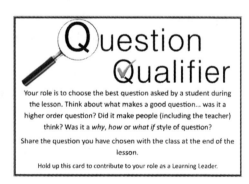

Question Qualifier

Your role is to choose the best question asked by a student during the lesson. Think about what makes a good question... was it a higher order question? Did it make people (including the teacher) think? Was it a *why*, *how* or *what if* style of question?

Share the question you have chosen with the class at the end of the lesson.

Hold up this card to contribute to your role as a Learning Leader.

Figure 4.4 Six Learning Leader cards (download the full set from the website)

Go Get Googler (active – as necessary)

In any lesson where students are encouraged to be inquisitive and explore the subject beyond the syllabus, there should be questions that neither the teacher nor the students can answer. . . but perhaps Google can! The Go Get Googler is the student who is tasked with finding out any information that is not readily available, but required by an individual or the whole class. The Go Get Googler could use a classroom computer, the teacher's laptop or perhaps his or her own device to search the Internet.

It is always useful to then follow up the discovery of any newfound information or answers by discussing its relevance, accuracy, reliability and, of course, how the information should be used.

Answer Analyst (active – end of a lesson)

The Answer Analyst is a student who is tasked with identifying the best answer offered by a student during the lesson. The Answer Analyst prompt card guides this student to think about what makes a good answer and to try and spot this during the lesson. The Answer Analyst will obviously pick up on the teacher's feedback and praise of answers during a lesson and this could help them select one answer for particular recognition. The Answer Analyst, along with a number of other roles, will hold up their card at the end of the lesson and share their choice with the rest of the class. Along with the Question Qualifier and Peer Praiser, this role helps the class recognise positive contributions and celebrate success.

Question Qualifier (active – end of a lesson)

Just like the Answer Analyst, the Question Qualifier is responsible for selecting and praising good examples. Learning is not a one-way process and students should be encouraged to pose their own questions, which facilitate deeper thinking. The Question Qualifier should look for examples of deeper thinking and higher-order questioning skills. The best examples might be those that made the whole class, including the teacher, think.

Wonder Worder (active – on mention of the Wonder Word)

The Wonder Worder role is used to encourage students to use key terminology and appropriate vocabulary during a lesson. The Wonder Worder chooses, or is assigned, a word or phrase based on the learning that took place in the previous few lessons (the Wonder Word). Their task is to listen out for the first student to use this phrase or word appropriately during the lesson. It is quite fun if this student has a buzzer or a bell they can ring to indicate that the Wonder Word has been spoken. The student who says the Wonder Word could then win a prize – a star, merit or even confectionery. A word to the wise – watch out for cases of sabotage where the Wonder Worder might leak the answer to a friend with designs on sharing the prize!

Skills Selector (active – start of a lesson or as necessary)

The Skills Selector is the student who is given the task of highlighting the key learning skills necessary for success in the lesson. The Skills Selector card suggests a range of skills that the student might nominate. The skill (or skills) should be those that the student believes are the most important for success in the activities being carried out during that lesson. For example, if the lesson requires the class to work in groups for any length of time the student might identify teamwork as the key skill for success. They would then go on to explain why they believe it is important and suggest what they could do to ensure their group works effectively as a team. The purpose of this is to get students thinking about their actions and behaviour. Other students could also be brought into this conversation to share their opinions. As the Skills Selector contributes to the lesson, so all other students will reflect on these skills, their own actions and their behaviour. At this point, it might be useful to show your class the Conditions for Learning Model (page 64) to encourage effective reflection and discussion.

Disposition Doctor (active – start of a lesson or as necessary)

The Disposition Doctor role works in exactly the same way as the Skills Selector. Indeed, it might be useful for these students to work together and discuss their ideas before addressing the class. Again, the Conditions for Learning Model will help the whole class reflect on the dispositions necessary for successful learning in their lesson.

Information Inquisition (active – end of a lesson)

Throughout the lesson, the Information Inquisition will have the task to consider two questions. How does what you have learnt today link to other topics, in this subject or any other? And what is the most important thing you have learnt today? In effect, these are questions that all students should consider, but the Information Inquisition will have the whole lesson to ponder these questions. As with the Skills Selector and Disposition Doctor, these questions can then be opened up for discussion with the whole class.

The Count (active – as necessary)

Counting down is an effective behaviour management strategy to get students listening. The premise is that all students are quiet, facing the front, looking and listening by the time you get to zero. I generally start at three, but five works just as well. Every student then has the time to hear the countdown, finish what they are doing and then conform. The Count is the student who will do this for you. When you are ready for the class to be quiet and listen, simply give your Count the nod for them to then start the countdown. The Count card gives this student advice on how to conduct the countdown, such as to count slowly and use half numbers if the class is particularly active, noisy or engaged in a task, or use positive reinforcement between numbers. If using The Count role, it might be necessary to choose students who you know have the confidence, and perhaps status, to carry it off. If you are adopting Learning Leaders with a more challenging class, you might want to avoid delegating classroom management strategies to your students, although you might be surprised how they respond to one another when behaviour and attention falls under their remit.

Giving The Count card to a particularly chatty or distracted student is one way to turn the most disruptive member of the class into your biggest advocate.

Peer Praiser (active – as necessary)

Unlike the Answer Analyst or the Question Qualifier, the Peer Praiser can give positive comments to any student for anything. This might be for a piece of work, for a positive contribution to a group or for helping another student. The Peer Praiser could share their praise at any point during the lesson by holding up their Learning Leader card. This strategy can work for any of your Learning Leaders when they wish to make a contribution relevant to their role. Alternatively you could ask the Peer Praiser to share their thoughts at the end of a lesson and comment on the actions or behaviour of several students. If you assign your Peer Praiser the task of commending other students' work, you might want to give them the freedom to move around the room during parts of the lesson.

Here I have offered 12 discrete roles that I find work for me, and if you like the concept, you may try all or a few of these out for yourself. The most important thing is to understand the principles on which these ideas are based: encouraging students to participate in meaningful discussions about learning and developing a unity between a teacher and his or her students.

Encouraging effective participation in group work

Five Group Roles

A team is often greater than the sum of its parts and this is just one reason to involve group work in classroom exercises. Students are often more engaged when working with their peers and through this process are able to learn from one another. One of the problems that could arise when students work in groups is that some have scope to opt out and disengage with the task or perhaps the quieter students are crowded out by those that are more confident or dominant. I have found that the larger the group, the more likely it is that one or more students will become, as is known in economics, 'free riders'.

Giving individuals a specific responsibility within a group is one way to challenge this and ensure all students are able to engage with the task. Designing roles for a task can be difficult and time consuming, so here are five generic roles that can contribute to effective group work.

- *Gatekeeper* – the student who is tasked with keeping the group focused and engaged in the task at hand.

- *Timekeeper* – the student who keeps track of time and reminds everyone of how long they have left.

- *Recorder* – the student who records ideas and decisions made by the group.

- *Checker* – the student who checks that objectives have been met, summarises outcomes and shares them with the class.

- *Sceptic* – the student who asks questions about how things could be done better, e.g. the task or interactions of the group.

What to do

- Display the group roles on the board or download the group role cards from the website. Print a set of cards for each group.

- Once these roles have been shared and explained with a class, students can either allocate the roles amongst themselves or they can be allocated by the teacher using group role cards. A third approach might be to get students to number themselves and then assign each number a role.

- Carry out the group activity and use the roles to positively reinforce instructions.

- The benefit of these roles is that they can be applied to any type of activity and ensure all students have a discrete area of responsibility that contributes to the success of the group.

Variations

Fewer roles can also be selected to match the size of the groups or additional roles can be created for larger groups. For example, the 'Checker' role can be split in two with a new 'Reporter' role being created. This student will take responsibility for feeding back to the class, whilst the Checker maintains the job of recording and checking decisions – you now have six group roles.

Applying these five/six group roles is also an effective classroom management technique.

Teaching tip

By observing how different groups are interacting and then announcing something like 'remember to keep your group on task, gatekeepers' will remind those students who fulfil this role, as well as everyone else, to focus on the task. This blanket instruction means you do not have to draw attention to one or two students who might be more interested in discussing the previous evening's footy scores.

Expert Groups

This activity comes under a number of guises, including 'home and away groups' and is particularly effective, not only because it ensures every student gains a specialism that their team will later rely on, but because it gets students moving around the room and working with a number of their peers. Expert Groups is a useful strategy to deploy when students are required to collect and use a variety of information to solve a task.

What to do

- Identify an activity that has 4–5 components. For example, five aspects of the body's respiratory system. Each aspect will form a specialist area that students will later become an 'expert' on. The number of components will also determine your group size.

- Allocate each student a letter and a number (A–E, 1–5).

- The first activity will involve students getting together into their numbered groups. These are the 'expert' or 'away' groups, in which they get together to complete a task in order to acquire knowledge on one of the components. In our example of the respiratory system, you might require experts on the throat, lungs and diaphragm.

- After completing their expert activity, students then regroup by letter – 'home groups' – where they share what they have learned whilst completing a second activity that requires input from each specialist.

Variations

Class sizes may not always permit an Expert Group activity, but a more flexible approach can be adopted. Instead, run an activity that requires students to find out additional information in order to complete it. Place these sources around the room (temporary wall displays can be effective) and get each group to designate a member to acquire the knowledge before returning to the group and disseminating the information. In this situation, perhaps only one or two students are required to be an expert and the task should be one that the group can continue to work on whilst some members are away becoming an expert.

Talking Tokens

Chips, counters or tokens can be used effectively in a range of contexts to encourage participation or limit the resources available to students (see also A Token Question, page 163). Talking Tokens can be used to encourage students to contribute to class or small group discussions. This approach is particularly useful during idea-generating sessions as it prevents the most outspoken students from dominating the activity.

What to do

- Allocate students tokens based on the minimum contributions you expect them to make.

- Explain that students must submit one of their tokens to a central pile every time they make a contribution, such as a new idea, an opinion or a solution. A token should not be submitted for simply saying something.

- Explain that every student should aim to have no tokens remaining by the end of the activity or lesson.

- Allocating different quantities of tokens can be an effective way to differentiate a task.

Teaching tip

Make it clear that students should not simply submit a token every time they say something. Lay down clear rules on what counts as a token. Advise your students that taking turns to share their ideas and opinions will be the most effective way to use their tokens.

Works well with

- Auction House (page 97)

- Group Work Pie Charts (page 72).

Composite Answers

This activity gets students collaborating to jointly produce an extended answer. A composite answer is one that is constructed through components of work produced by several students. The benefit of working in this way is that it allows students to be exposed to each other's work, gets them analysing and evaluating ideas and focuses their attention on the key features of a good answer.

What to do

- Set an extended writing task, such as a longer written answer or essay question, that all students complete individually.

- Put students into small groups of threes or fours and ask them to discuss what makes a good answer. Students could use a marking rubric or mark scheme to do this.

- Set each group the challenge of producing a joint answer using at least one component from each student.

- Ask each group to read their Composite Answer and explain why each component was chosen.

- Different colours or fonts could be used to highlight which aspects have been used from each student.

Teaching tip

A Composite Answer activity can be used as a follow-up to a piece of home-work. Working in small groups, students will analyse and evaluate their answers together. In carrying out a Composite Answer, students will receive quality peer feedback, and perhaps, from time to time, remove the need for the work to be marked by their teacher.

Works well with

- Comprehension Cranium (page 88)

- Creativity Carousel (page 133).

Structures for learning together

Student Tutors

The Learning Pyramid, as accredited to the National Training Labs,[2] suggests, and it is widely accepted, that students retain 90 per cent of what they learn when they are involved in coaching and teaching that learning to others. It would therefore make sense for our students to adopt this approach whenever possible.

Adopting Student Tutors involves using students who have acquired a certain mastery of a concept, process or skill to support other students. We have all had those lessons where we can't get around students fast enough to provide them with additional support and this technique is in direct response to those situations. Using Student Tutors involves assigning a small number of students the role of tutor with a particular focus over a set period of time. For example, a student might be assigned the role of Student Tutor if they are able to interpret a piece of comprehension in a Spanish lesson, have an aptitude for algebra or are able to demonstrate a skill or technique in PE.

There are three benefits to operating with Student Tutors:

1. It nurtures a culture of support and collaboration in your classroom.

2. The Student Tutor gets status for supporting other pupils and consolidates their own understanding.

3. The teacher has more time to assess progress and facilitate the whole class.

Figure 4.5   Student Tutor card

What to do

- The role of Student Tutor can be assigned by handing out the Student Tutor card (Figure 4.5). I have found that pupils particularly like it when the card is placed on a lanyard so they can wear it around their necks!

- It helps to announce to the class that, for example, 'Charlotte is now a Student Tutor for plate tectonics for the next ten minutes. She will come and support anyone who is stuck.' Not only does this give Charlotte status, but for a defined period of time she is now able to get out of her seat and 'tutor' other students in the class.

- It helps to involve all students in the role of Student Tutor and not just the most able.

Variations

Another approach is to award the role of Student Tutor to a student who has produced a particularly good piece of work. The Student Tutor card then lets them share their best practice with others. This will help other students appreciate the success criteria and understand what a good one looks like (WAGOLL).

Silent Galleries

This activity lets students learn from each other's work and encourages a collaborative sharing culture. In a Silent Gallery, students move around the room, in silence, looking at the work completed by fellow students laid out on desks or stuck to the wall. This activity might last for up to ten minutes, depending on the size of the class and nature of the work.

What to do

- One approach is to use a Silent Gallery as an assessment and rewards strategy. As students circulate the room, they are required to allocate three awards to other students' work.

- Students allocate their award by drawing a symbol on the corner of the work to represent the award they are giving. If students writing on each other's work is not desirable, an alternative approach is to use post-it notes or stickers. For example, three awards I have used in the past include the most original idea (light-bulb), the most practical solution (spanner) and the piece of work that shows the most effort (a star). Each student is only allowed to award one of each category and cannot give any to themselves.

- The nature of the awards can be tailored to suit any subject and at the end of the activity the winners are those who receive the most symbols. The teacher can then bring these pieces of work to the front of the class and lead a discussion on why these pieces of work are successful.

Variations

A second approach to a Silent Gallery is to use it as an information-sharing exercise. Organise different groups of students to complete a piece of work on a different topic. This could be a research activity where each group becomes an expert on a certain aspect of a subject and then produces a visual piece of work, such as a poster or wall display. The Silent Gallery will then involve each group circulating the room to collect information from other groups' displays. This could be organised by handing each group a set of questions or a fact sheet they have to complete as they move around the room. This is a great way to use students as experts and is effective for sharing lots of information.

Think–Pair–Square–Share

A well-known and staple strategy for encouraging group discussions before answering a question is the Think–Pair–(Square)–Share approach. A question is posed to the class. Individuals are then given 30–60 seconds to think in silence. Students then turn to discuss their ideas with the student sat next to them for a further 30–60 seconds. The 'square' step is optional and dependent on the size and layout of your classroom. Each pair will turn to another pair and discuss their answers. A traditional classroom layout might allow students to work with the table in front or behind (making a square). Once more, allow 30–60 seconds. At this point, all students should have at least one idea from their small group discussion so the teacher might opt to direct a question, such as, 'Saskia, tell me what your group thought is', therefore sharing their answer/s with the rest of the class. This technique helps students develop their initial ideas further and lowers the chance of individuals not being able to respond. It will also avoid the scenario of the teacher taking an answer within the first few seconds from the student quickest to raise their hand.

Quiz Quiz Trade (QQT)

This is a nice little active revision strategy that gets your students circulating the class, sharing ideas and questioning each other. The name of this activity was coined by Dr Spencer Kagan as a cooperative learning structure.[3]

What to do

- Each student is given a card with a question on it. This can be as simple or as complex as you like, but the answer should have a relatively short response in the form of a statement or a set of bullet points. The answers can be written on the cards or time can be given for students to find out the answer and write it on the card themselves, prior to starting the Quiz Quiz Trade (QQT).

- All students are then told to move around the room and form pairs. As students pair up, they will take it in turn to quiz one another. The correct answers can then be shared once each student has attempted to answer the other student's question.

- Once each student has quizzed the other, the cards are traded and students then find another partner. Your class continues this process until everyone has answered each question. Note that students are likely to trade back a question that they have already answered towards the end of this activity, but this does not matter. The swapping of the cards helps will memory as your students will ask and answer each question.

Teaching tip

Number the questions on each card as this helps students to find the questions that they have not already answered.

Speed Dating

Aptly named for the way students move around the classroom, and nothing else, this approach to collaborative learning is similar to QQT. As with QQT, each student is assigned an area of specialism that they will share with other students in exchange for reciprocal information. This approach is particularly useful when you require your class to take in a large amount of information.

What to do

- Allocate each student a concept or topic to focus on and give them time to become familiar with it. Encourage students to create their own notes to condense and summarise the topic. This could be a template of features or points to include, or as simple as three bullet points.

- Arrange students into one of the two systems below; they will then get to 'date' each other in a carousel to share information. Students will move to a new partner based on a timer set by the teacher – for example, every 3–4 minutes, taking it in turn to explain their topic.

- System 1: the dinner party (everyone meets everyone) – organise your class so that students are sitting along a long table facing each other, with even numbers on either side and no one sitting at either end (Figure 4.6). Students will then rotate in one direction around the table until they have sat opposite everyone else. If you have an odd number of students, have each student sit out one turn or join in the activity yourself.

- System 2: inner and outer circles (double the roles) – if you don't have enough topics to allocate each student their own, you can easily double up the roles. Put students into two groups – A and B. Each topic will be covered

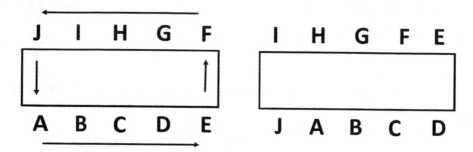

Figure 4.6   System 1 table layout: the dinner party

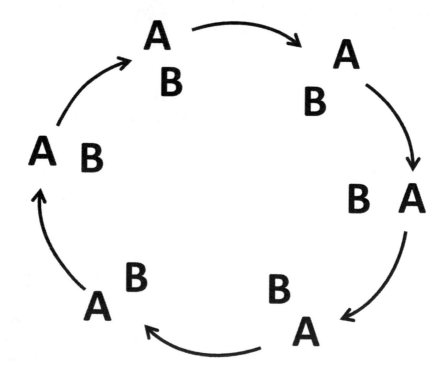

Figure 4.7   System 2 table layout: inner and outer circles

by one student in each group. Arrange Group A and Group B into an inner and an outer circle (Figure 4.7). As and Bs will face each other at the start by sitting opposite the student with the same topic. Bs will then rotate around the circle every few minutes until they arrive back in their original seat.

- At the end of the speed dating activity, all students have covered a range of topics and produced a comprehensive set of notes.

Four-way Worksheets

A Four-way Worksheet is a tool that will get your students collaborating in a circle and helping each other solve problems. The purpose of the exercise is for a group of four students to successfully answer four related questions or solve four problems together.

What to do

- Download the Four-way Worksheet template from the website.

- Complete the worksheet by adding four questions or problems. These can be separate or related.

- Students will work in groups of four around a small table and attempt to complete one of the questions in a set time.

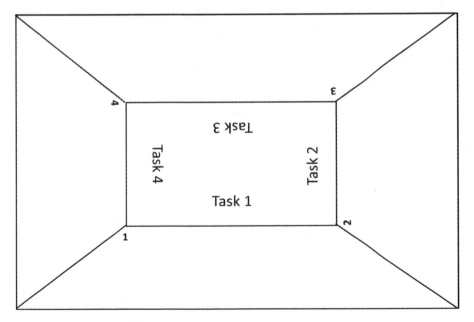

Figure 4.8 Four-way Worksheet

- Once the time is up, 1s work with 2s and 3s work with 4s to discuss their question. After a short period of time, stop the discussion and swap partners: 1s work with 4s and 2s work with 3s.

- Following these discussions, students spend a few minutes improving their own answers or make changes to their solution.

Variation

An alternative approach is to get each student to read their question/problem and then discuss the answer/solution with two partners before attempting their answer.

Debates

Whether or not your school has a debating society, adopting some of the simple principles from a debating structure is an effective way to get students thinking systematically, developing their analysis and evaluation skills, whilst at the same time incorporating an element of competition. There are many structures and systems for debates; however, below is a simple approach that could easily fit into one lesson. The strict timings of a debate will add a formal air to the proceedings and avoid an unstructured argument taking place.

Eight-minute Introduction to issue or resolution (teacher or student-led)

Six-minute Position Presentation – affirmative team

Six-minute Position Presentation – opposing team

Five-minute work period

Three-minute Rebuttal – affirmative team

Three-minute Rebuttal – opposing team

Two-minute work period

Three-minute Response – opposing team

Three-minute Response – affirmative team

One-minute work period

Two-minute Position Summary – opposing team

Two-minute Position Summary – affirmative team

Announcement of Winner

What to do

- Set the debating topic prior to the lesson when the debate will take place. Organise the class into two groups and give them time to research and prepare their case. This could be lesson time or as a homework activity.

- (optional) On the day of the debate ask your students to attend the lesson in business attire. This will add to the formal proceedings.

- Organise your classroom so that the two debating teams are facing one another and follow the timings above.

- Recording the debate on video can act as a very effective source of revision that can be posted on the school VLE.

Teaching tip

To ensure each student contributes towards the debate, use a technique such as Talking Tokens (page 124). You can even incorporate the tokens into the scoring system at the end of the debate, by counting up the tokens from each student who has made a contribution.

Creativity Carousel

A Creativity Carousel can be used in any creative lesson where students are required to come up with ideas and designs, such as Art or Design Technology. Using a mood board (which is an inspirational collage showing the theme and colour scheme of a project), the class come up with a range of unique and innovative designs for each other's projects.

What to do

- Each pupil is given a piece of A4/A3 paper, which they split into 6–12 equal sections (dependent on time). The teacher then asks the pupil to draw their original design idea in the first box.

- Pupils then move around the classroom and sit at somebody else's design sheet and mood board. Allow students to study the mood boards for about 20–30 seconds before asking them to begin.

- Using a pen (not a pencil, as it stops pupils from rubbing out) and a time limit of 1–2 minutes (you can tell what amount of time is required after the first design), pupils have to come up with a design in one of the boxes, based on the mood board in front of them. Encourage them to add as much detail as possible, including relevant annotations.

- Give a countdown of the time throughout each design rotation. Using music is an effective technique as this helps students concentrate and the music can be stopped to signify a rotation.

- As this task progresses, it gradually gets more difficult to come up with an idea that hasn't already been drawn; this is when the teacher should start giving them some guidance. For example:

  o Combine two of the ideas on the sheet into one unique design.

  o Enlarge one of the sections of a previous design.

  o Minimise one of the sections of a previous design.

  o Remove a section of a design and replace with something new.

  o Pretend you are Lady Gaga's designer. What ideas would she come up with?

Students will enjoy seeing their design sheets at the end of the activity when they return to their places and are faced with a variety of new and innovative designs to take forward (for example, see Figure 4.9).

Pass the Parcel Essay Writing

The activity will encourage students to build an extended answer from an initial statement. Students will develop their writing skills and the activity can be

Figure 4.9 Example from a Creativity Carousel

used as an effective revision exercise. The activity can start with multiple statements, which are passed around the classroom simultaneously.

What to do

- Start the activity by asking each student to write down a statement relating to the topic. For example, 'All members of a society should be given the right to vote'. In order to ensure breadth and variety, these initial statements could be provided by the teacher – one per student or pair.

- Each student/pair is then required to add a new point to the answer. It is useful to provide students with a structure so that all answers are complete at the end of the activity. Using a clear structure will also help students learn how to form their answers. For example, a six-step approach is suggested below.

- By the end of the activity, a range of answers has been collaboratively produced by the class. These can now be shared and discussed.

1. Statement of fact or opinion.

2. Describe/Explain – *This means that. . . This is because. . .*

3. Develop the point – *Furthermore. . . As a result. . . Consequently. . .*

4. Example / Evidence – *For example. . . We know this because. . .*

5. Counteract / Criticise – *However. . . On the other hand. . . but. . .*

6. Conclusion / Judgement – *In summary. . . Overall. . . to conclusion. . .*

Ask the Teacher

As with A Token Question (page 163), this activity will help build independence amongst students. The idea is for students to work together to identify the key questions they want answering before they attempt a task.

What to do

- Decide on the number of questions that students are able to ask the teacher before starting a task. Once these questions have been asked, no other questions can be directed at the teacher.

- Students work in small groups to come up with 3–4 questions that they would like answering.

- Once groups have decided on their questions, they each take it in turns to ask one question, which the teacher will then attempt to answer. This continues with each group until the quota has been reached.

- This approach works particularly well when students are given a problem to solve.

Top ten digital tools for collaborative learning

In this section, you will find references to many exciting and effective apps, websites and resources that teachers and students can use to support learning. However, the purpose of this section is not simply to identify the best digital tools currently available for use in education. Digital tools are constantly evolving and there are a myriad of websites and blogs that provide a comprehensive overview with opinions on the best – The Centre for Learning and Performance Technologies is one such site that annually updates its 'Top 100 Tools for Learning'.[4] Instead, this list will explore ten ways in which digital tools can, and already do, change the way we teach and learn. Indeed, these ten approaches not only offer opportunities to do things better, but they also allow us to modify and redefine teaching and learning and do things that were previously not possible.[5]

1. Flipping

At the start of this chapter, we discussed the growth of the flipped classroom as an approach to teaching and learning, how it allows teachers to facilitate problem-solving during their lessons and how digital tools are making it easier to acquire knowledge beyond the classroom. Flipping the classroom becomes increasingly accessible as new sources, such as blogs and instructional videos, spring up on the web. There is a wide range of tools that allow educators to master the flipped classroom by creating their own bespoke tutorials that can be shared with students. Two apps that are fantastic at doing this, amongst others, are **Explain Everything** and **Educreations**. Both provide a means to record tutorials on an interactive whiteboard where images can be manipulated and annotated. These can then be shared with students through a school VLE or video sharing site. Tutorial videos can just as easily be produced with screen casting software and shared in the same way – **Jing** is just one highly rated piece of software that can do the job. All of these tools can help teachers produce highly effective resources to support students, and the ease of using these tools means they are no longer only the tenure of the tech-savvy teachers amongst us. The real benefits of these tools begin to pay dividends when students start creating their own tutorials for each other.

2. Curating

Send your students to research a topic, to find real-world examples, ideas for inspiration or the opinions of experts, and the quantity of information readily available is overwhelming. Our job, as educators, is now less about providing students with the information they need and more about helping them filter, sort and identify the value of the information they are able to access. There are many tools that can help our students bring useful information together in one place that they can then learn from, use and distribute to others. **Scoop.it** is a site that allows users to find things, organise them, add their own opinions and ideas and share them with the world. Users can also access the community of active curators who share an interest in their topic. Virtual bulletin boards are another great way for students to collect ideas, identify useful sources and build a big picture of their learning. Tools such as **Pinterest, Pearltrees** and **Popplet** all have their relative merits. These tools are effective at constructing a bank of shared knowledge that can be used as a link to further reading and revision or even building an entire virtual course.

3. Hosting

Many of the tools mentioned in this section remove the boundaries and restraints of traditional forms of learning. No longer do our students have to conform to the place, period or pace we set. However, there are times when, as teachers, we want to take control and conduct things in a more structured manner. It is likely that at some point you have taken part in an online training event held through webinar software, such as **Adobe Connect** or **Blackboard Collaborate**. These are just two examples of tools that can be used as a 'virtual classroom', with a wide range of tools to share resources, present and annotate information and communicate in real time with our students. I have used webinar software to conduct revision booster sessions the night before a big exam to help reassure students and field any last-minute questions and I have seen a Head of Year use the same software to carry out live form-time quizzes from the comfort of his office with 12 tutor groups at the same time who were scattered across the school.

4. Networking

The wealth of opportunities to use social media sites such as **Facebook** and **Twitter** is endless, provided we have provisions and policies to counteract the pitfalls. On a basic level, departmental or subject accounts can be set up and used to easily broadcast messages and develop subject conversations beyond the classroom. Social media allows us to access learning on a virtual level, but more importantly on a global level. Information, conversations and ideas are no longer restricted to those students within your class, but can be shared with anyone around the world. There are fantastic examples of teachers and students using Twitter not only to 'eavesdrop' on global trends, but actively engage industry experts in virtual debates. This is certainly redefining teaching and learning and an easy starting point might be to start following subject-specific hashtags such as #Engchat, #Scichat, #STEM or #Mathchat. Why not have a go at starting a lesson, not only with an objective but with a custom hashtag, and see where it takes you? You can even effectively visualise and project tweets based around a hashtag with one of the many Twitter Wall web apps, such as **TweetBeam** or **Visible Tweets**. If you are looking for a more secure way to collaborate with your students, **Edmodo** offers many of the functions offered by the other tools mentioned in this section, including the ability to set tasks, manage projects, submit work and monitor progress in a secure and social learning environment.

5. Contributing

A particular benefit of technology is that it encourages students to contribute to a discussion or piece of work when they might not have been willing to put their hand up during a lesson. Networking tools are great for achieving this, but these tools are particularly effective at allowing discussions and analysis to take place around a central theme such as an idea, a question or a piece of work. Unlike networking tools, they are generally closed to a user-defined group, such as a class. **VoiceThread** is one tool that lets its users couple together images and videos with annotations and/or comments. We will explore the value of quality feedback in Chapter 6, but imagine having a piece of homework that not only you can comment on and share back with the student, but every student in your class. . . another class. . . or next year! Concept mapping tools are another way to go, as they allow students to simultaneously bring together images, text and videos all at the same time. **Popplet** and **Padlet** are two examples of websites/apps that allow for collaboration and negotiation to take place – anytime, anywhere.

6. Interacting

There are some great tools that allow students to interact with information and create their own interactive resources. **Aurasma** is a website that offers an augmented reality platform. The technology can link an aura – any rich media such an image or video – to a 2D or 3D object that can be triggered by a smartphone or tablet device with a camera. Basically, the software can recognise a 'trigger image' set as a picture or an object. It will then overlay media on top of the image when

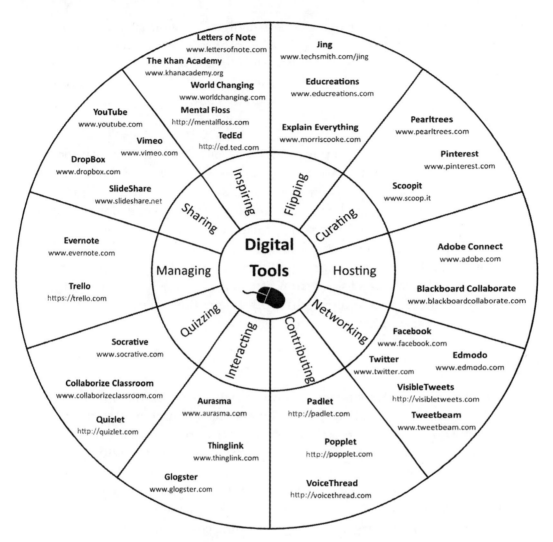

Figure 4.10 Digital tools for learning

viewed through the camera of a smartphone or tablet. If that made no sense, visit the website to see how it works – it's quite magical! Aurasma offers a multitude of applications in an educational setting, which are only restricted to your imagination. For example, send your students on an interactive treasure hunt or fact-finding mission around the school or a famous landmark. Picture a wall of historical figures that come to life and talk to the students when viewed through the camera of a device, or a library where the book covers trigger a video book review from fellow students – just a few ideas that augmented reality can make possible.

There are other ways that we can engage our students and get them interacting with information. **ThingLink** and **Glogster** are two sources that let users create a digital paper, bringing together digital content such as images, text, interactive graphics and links to websites. The content can then be shared with others or embedded into a website. Both tools also offer users the ability to search for content created by other teachers and students in a public domain.

7. Quizzing

Although I have referred to this category as 'quizzing', these digital tools offer much more than that. **Socrative** is a web-based tool that lets teachers engage students in a range of exercises and collate the responses for formative assessment. You can ask questions in the moment via single-question activities, or design a quiz beforehand and run it during the lesson. Either way, you will be able to visualise and measure student understanding in real time. **Quizlet** is another site that offers similar capabilities, but also lets teachers and students create digital flashcards for revision. If you are looking for a dedicated place to hold class discussions and debates, **Collaborize Classroom** is a tool similar to Edmodo that also offers a comprehensive range of functions.

8. Managing

If you teach a creative subject or adopt project-based learning, there is a range of digital tools that can help your students organise and manage their projects effectively. As more and more schools move to a 1:1 approach with ICT devices, there will be a greater need for students to move away from traditional organisation systems, such as books and folders, in favour of digital solutions. **Evernote** allows students to organise documents, capture images, record audio messages and take down notes. Tags can be added to entries and Evernote will even pick out words from an image, making everything completely searchable. **Trello** is another project management tool that lets users organise a project using moveable cards on a pin board. A range of features lets these cards be commented on by others, organised by colour and rearranged into different categories.

9. Sharing

With the growing potential to create digital content comes the need to store it somewhere where it can be accessed by all. The ability to embed digital content into any web-based tool means that we can make everything accessible at one point of entry. Most of the tools mentioned above make this possible. Teachers, departments and schools can easily set up their own dedicated **YouTube** channels and just as effective are other video-sharing sites, such as **Vimeo**. Presentations and teaching notes can also be made extremely accessible through tools such as

Dropbox and **SlideShare**, all of which become accessible through the click of a smartphone camera (see 'A Quick Response', page 145).

10. Inspiring

The web offers tons of ways to engage students in our subjects. Inspire them with talks and interviews from some of the world's leading experts on all manner of subjects with sites such as **Ted-Ed** and **The Khan Academy** (see Ten Minutes of TED, page 100). There are also many ways to encourage deeper thinking and stimulate debate with various sources on the web. Both **The Telegraph** and **The Guardian** post 'pictures of the week', which can be used to get students thinking. One idea might be to select an image from either site's list during a registration period and ask you students to come up with the '5Ws' – an engaging start to the day or a great early-bird activity for a lesson. **Mental Floss** is another site that poses interesting questions, problems and weird, funny and wonderful things – great as a source of 'Thunks'.[6] If you are looking for interesting and thought-provoking articles to inspire your students, look no further than **Letters of Note**, a site that has collated interesting letters, notes, postcards and telegrams from famous people in history, or **World Changing**, a source of ideas, innovations and projects to improve our world.

Chapter summary

In this chapter, we have explored ways to share the responsibility of learning with students, such as Learning Leaders and Student Tutors, and highlighted ways to encourage participation, such as Group Roles and Composite Answers. Working collaboratively allows students to access one another as sources of information, support and guidance, and many of the digital tools discussed in this chapter open up opportunities for this to happen beyond the classroom.

Successful collaboration takes time to nurture. Students need to feel safe in their environment and respected as essential contributors to the learning of the whole class. In order to achieve this, students must see the value in learning together and the importance of the interpersonal skills discussed in Chapter 2. This is why it is always important for students to reflect on the process of their learning whenever they work in groups and teams. Collaborative learning brings with it its own challenges, but the benefits far outweigh any costs when learning becomes a social process through which students gain from one another. Ultimately, collaborative approaches to learning are some of the best levers we have as educators to facilitate the learning process.

Notes

1   The flipped approach to teaching is where students learn new content outside of the lesson, usually by watching an online video, providing more time in lessons to focus on problems, enquiry and guided tuition. See *Flip Your Classroom: Teach Every Student in Every Classroom Every Day* (Bergmann & Sams, 2012).

2   NTL Institute for Applied Behavioral Science, 300 N. Lee Street, Suite 300, Alexandria, VA 22314. 1-800-777-5227. http://homepages.gold.ac.uk/polovina/learn-pyramid/about.htm.

3   Kagan Structures for Collaborative Learning cover a wide range of approaches to classroom practice: www.kaganonline.com.

4   The Centre for Learning and Performance Technologies (http://c4lpt.co.uk/) conducts an annual survey of professionals in education and learning industries and publishes a top 100 ranking of digital tools for learning, with information and comments from the voters.

5   The idea that technology can lead to the modification or redefinition of teaching and learning is taken from Dr Ruben Puentedura's SAMR Model (www.hippasus.com), which aims to help educators integrate technology into the learning process.

6   A thunk is a question that challenges you to think about the world in a whole new light. See *The Little Book of Thunks* by Ian Gilbert (2007).

5 Challenge and support

For me, differentiating learning and meeting the needs of individuals within my classes has always seemed to be my biggest challenge as a teacher, especially as the majority of my experience has come from teaching mixed-ability groups with a full spectrum of abilities. I remember a conversation I had with my line manager at my first school after he had carried out one of my first formal lesson observations as an NQT. He believed my lesson was 'clearly differentiated', and so it should have been – I had spent hours the night before preparing my lesson, making sure the needs of every student (three or four in particular) were being met by the activities, gradation of questions and bespoke resources I would be using. The lesson went well and the feedback helped satisfy my self-esteem and justify the hours I had put in to planning and preparing the lesson. In our post-observation feedback, I had tried to make the point that the effort that had gone into the lesson was in no way sustainable, lesson by lesson. All I got from my line manager was some sympathy, but little in the way of an answer. Fortunately, in time, I learnt that effective differentiation need not be so time and resource intensive.

The three most common approaches for differentiating learning are often referred to as 'by task', 'by outcome' and 'by resource'. However, this is sometimes easier said than done. If we are to differentiate by task, then how do we manage multiple activities at once? If by resource, then where do I

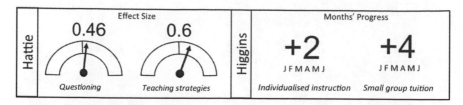

Figure 5.1 The capacity for a teacher to challenge and support all students is their ability to differentiate learning. This chapter includes a variety of approaches to achieve the strategies referenced above.

find time to prepare multiple materials? And if by outcome, then should I just expect some students to do more and others less? These are some of the issues we will explore in this chapter, with some practical strategies to answer these questions.

Ultimately, differentiation is about playing the long game, not about different activities and resources, but about knowing your students, challenging them and supporting them with the right questions, quality marking, constructive feedback and the opportunities to self-assess and set their own targets. These things don't happen in one lesson, but over the course of a term or a year. It is the little interactions we have with our students lesson by lesson, week by week, that help us meet their needs.

Figure 5.2 illustrates the ways in which we differentiate learning for our students. Although it is common to design and plan unique tasks and resources for students at either end of the spectrum, the majority of the work we do to differentiate learning is far subtler and seldom requires additional planning and preparation.

In this section, you will find strategies that will make differentiation a little easier, whether you are looking to personalise the learning experience, facilitate choice and flexibility, or meet their needs through questioning. Consequently, these strategies should help you find the right balance of challenge and support so that every student is working at the right level – just beyond their comfort zone.

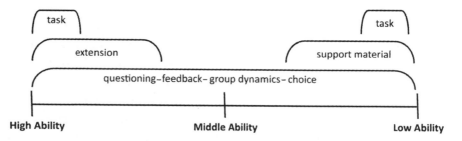

Figure 5.2   Differentiation spectrum

Challenging students through extension activities

Extension activities should offer students different and more challenging work that pushes them on to learn something new, improve their skills or create something to support their learning, such as revision material. Activities cease to be an extension when they simply offer more of the same.

A Quick Response

QR codes (quick response codes) were first introduced for the automotive industry and are barcodes consisting of black modules (square dots) arranged in a square grid on a white background. These can be read by an imaging device such as a camera on a smartphone. They are most commonly seen in magazines and advertising billboards, as a tool for consumers to scan and access a company's website, but they have a useful application in the twenty-first century classroom.

As more and more schools move towards a bring-your-own-device (BYOD) policy and as portable devices, such as tablet computers, become more common, so these little square barcodes will play a part in allowing students to access additional content. Where students have access to their own, or even a school's, portable device, the QR code can be used to differentiate lessons, providing additional challenge or support. QR codes provide a means for students to be working on different tasks at different times throughout a lesson. The most common use of a QR code is to link to a URL address, but they can also be used to return a text or audio message.

What to do

- QR codes are free to generate. Use a website such as http://qrcode.kaywa. com to create your codes and download the images to use in presentations, worksheets and displays.

- QR codes can be read by a smartphone or tablet device with a barcode scanner application. There are many good, and free, scanner apps that can be downloaded for any platform.

- Another really useful website is www.qrstuff.com – this website allows you to use QR codes in a variety of ways. For example, create codes of different colours, generate a text response or geo-locate an address on Google Maps.

Variations

- Add a QR code to a worksheet or presentation which links to a resource such as a video clip from YouTube, TeacherTube, etc. Students can then scan the code to watch the video immediately or at a later date. Videos can be selected to support students when they are stuck or to challenge students through an extension activity (watch the clip and answer a question). Watching a video in a lesson normally means everyone has to stop what they are doing and watch it at the same time. With a QR code, students can scan and watch the video whenever they choose.

- Colour-coordinating QR codes can make for an effective approach to differentiation. Different colours can be used to provide instructions for different groups or learners. Different colours can represent various levels of support – for example, to give students hints and tips on completing a task. The QR code in Figure 5.3 will provide you with a simple audio message. (www.qrvoice.com)

- QRSTUFF (www.qrstuff.com) is a site that allows you to create QR codes that convert text into audio. These QR codes can then be placed in books, worksheets and presentations – a fun way to give instructions, or perhaps, an option for supporting EAL students?

Figure 5.3   Example of a QR code with audio

Figure 5.4   Example of a QR code with a geo-location address

- A text or audio response can also be used as a fun way to ensure students engage with feedback from a piece of homework.

- QRStuff (www.qrstuff.com) will also generate a geo-location address. This is a great way to show students geographical locations – experience visiting a location without the expense of a field trip. Students can also drop in to explore the location with Street View on Google Maps. See where the code in Figure 5.4 takes you!

- Use a QR code that links to a Dropbox folder (www.dropbox.com) so that students can download your lesson notes. This saves time handing notes out and makes it easy for students to locate them on a school network or managed learning environment (MLE).

- A QR code can also be used to link students to a regular source of information, such as a subject page in a MLE. An alternative to this is to create your own winksite. Here teachers can create their own mobile website and community. Each site can contain ten pages and include blogs, forums and surveys, amongst other useful tools. I use a winksite to share homework with my students. Sticking a QR code on the inside of their exercise books means they never have an excuse to forget the homework that I post on my winksite.

Bloom's Challenge Wall

Whether we use Bloom's Taxonomy of Learning Domains as an explicit tool to elicit higher-order thinking or questioning or implicitly to assess progress against a mark scheme, it is a useful model to plan and design learning activities. One way to apply Bloom's Taxonomy could be to design a predefined bank of extension activities. Bloom's Challenge Wall provides students with a range of extension activities for producing something useful that will aid their learning. These ideas are built around the six revised stages of Bloom's Taxonomy and can be used to provide challenge at different stages of the learning journey. For example, an extension challenge for students in the first lesson of a new topic might simply be to come up with an acronym to summarise their knowledge or produce a simple revision card. A more advanced challenge might be to come up with, and solve, a problem based on the concept being studied. Figure 5.5 illustrates an example of a challenge wall with activities linked to the six stages of Bloom's Taxonomy.

What to do

- Download the example of Bloom's Challenge Wall from the website, or create your own with generic activities suitable for your subject.

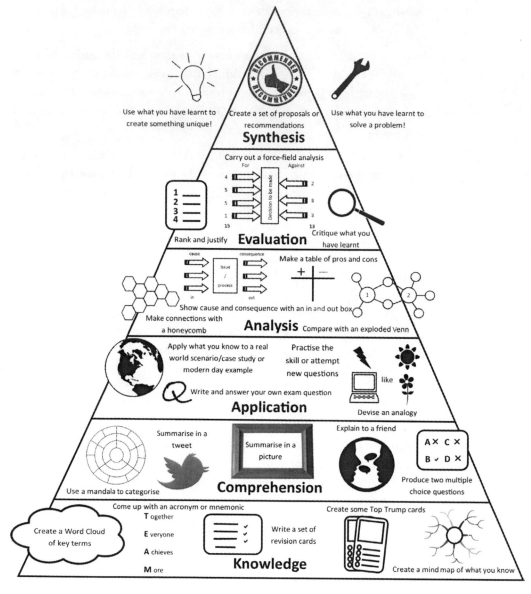

Figure 5.5 Bloom's Challenge Wall

- Display the Challenge Wall in your classroom or get students to stick it into their exercise books.

- When students are ready to move onto an extension activity, ask them to choose an appropriate challenge from the wall.

Variations

A Challenge Wall could also act as the basis for a homework menu system or simply to provide students with a choice of tasks. Why not allocate points to the different challenges as part of a reward system?

Teaching tip

Students can be guided towards an extension activity based on the teacher's assessment of their understanding. For example, at the start of a new topic it might be more appropriate for students to attempt challenges from the bottom of the pyramid.

Works well with

- Taking the Credit (page 159)
- Challenge Corner (below).

Challenge Corner

An effective way to use the learning environment is to create an area where students can go to access extension materials and stimulus. This area, or zone, within a classroom could be a display (Challenge Wall) or corner of the room (Challenge Corner) where students go, sit next to, or collect work from in order to access extension tasks, material or ideas. Here are a few suggestions to help teachers create an effective extension zone in their classrooms.

What to do

- Remember that the purpose of extension is not 'more of the same' and students must see any extension as an opportunity to push themselves. The activities involved in a Challenge Zone must create these opportunities if students are to aspire to it.

- A Challenge Zone could provide students with an opportunity to apply their understanding in different contexts. For example, this could involve the application of scientific concepts to various real-world problems. A Challenge Wall could therefore include case studies and problems for students to apply.

- Use a Challenge Zone to get students to come up with their own extension questions to encourage higher-order thinking. One way to do this would be to display the Question Matrix (see page 55) – students can use the suggested question stems to form extensions for discussion in small groups.

- Set your Challenge Zone up with a range of creative activities to apply their understanding. For example, making a set of revision cards, an acronym or mnemonic to remember the topic or creating an artefact based on the topic. Bloom's Challenge Wall could be displayed as a poster to give students ideas on what to do.

- Encourage students to make connections with other areas of the syllabus by placing an envelope of key words/topics on hexagonal cards on the wall. Students can then use these to pick out the topic they have studied and place related topics together. This will encourage 'relational learning' and help students understand the 'big picture' on how your subject interlinks.

Variations

Extension can also be an opportunity for students to find out about further areas of study. Locate GCSE or A Level articles in the Challenge Zone so that students can explore your subject at a higher level. For example, a Challenge Zone could be located next to the shelf where you keep GCSE/A level or even degree level texts, articles and magazines.

Challenge Envelope

It is surprising the effect it can have when you put something in an envelope. All of a sudden the item becomes a little bit more mystical and secretive (or is that just me?). When planning a discrete extension activity, it is useful to create a Challenge Envelope. A Challenge Envelope is a secret task that you place in an envelope and stick to your board or display somewhere in the room.

What to do

- Make up a Challenge Envelope and stick it near the teacher's board at the front of the classroom. Place a suitable extension task and the necessary resources inside the envelope.

- When students are ready, they can collect the activity or instructions from the envelope. You can build this up with your class – 'Who will be the first to discover the contents of the Challenge Envelope?' This adds a bit of kudos for the students who complete their work and then take up the challenge.

- The extension tasks inside the envelope can be specific to the topic being learnt, or more open and generic. More generic activities, such as creating quizzes or a set of Top Trump cards, can be left in the envelope and used with a range of classes, rotating the challenge every so often.

Variations

Different coloured envelopes could also be adopted to represent contrasting levels of difficulty or types of activity.

Teaching tip

It is important to ensure these extension tasks are creative, and perhaps include an aspect of fun, if your students are going to want to open the envelope and engage with what's inside.

Secret Mission

Envelopes can also be used to distribute secret missions to your class. Unlike the Challenge Envelope, the Secret Mission is targeted at individuals. A Secret Mission can help you differentiate learning at any level and tailor an activity to the needs of specific students. For example, giving a student an additional, and perhaps deeper, question for them to answer, getting a student to focus on a specific weakness (e.g. spelling), or simply challenging a quiet student to make three positive contributions during the lesson. Students enjoy receiving a personalised mission and can become quite excited to find one on, or under, their chair as they enter the room.

What to do

- Place a Secret Mission inside an envelope or simply on a piece of paper and stick it to the bottom of a student's chair.

- It is rarely possible to give a Secret Mission to every student in your class, so perhaps plan to write three per lesson, based on the targets of individuals, and rotate the students who receive them each lesson.

- Collect the slips of paper or envelopes that you wrote the Secret Missions on at the end of the lesson. You can then write a message to each student praising them on how they performed.

Teaching tip

It sometimes helps to base the mission on a recent piece of homework or observation you made about a student – this makes the mission more personal and relevant.

Thinking Extension

The last thing the winner of a burger-eating contest wants is to win a free burger. . . or any other form of food for that matter. So why should our students want to attempt more questions when they have completed the tasks you set the class? Instead, make your extensions thinking extensions. A thinking extension is a question that you might write on the whiteboard, include in a slideshow or write at the bottom of a worksheet. Instead of writing an answer to this question, students are expected to reflect on its meaning and possible answers. Philosophical questions often work best as a thinking extension or any other higher-order question, with stems such as 'what if. . .', 'why should. . .', 'how might. . .', etc.

Works well with

- The Socratic Plenary (page 52)
- The Q-Matrix (page 55).

Personalised learning

If we are to personalise learning, we must first understand our students. Much of what we do to personalise learning comes from the choices we give students and the questions we ask. However, these next two strategies are about designing your lessons to the interests of your students.

Accelerated Learning Contracts

Whatever the context of your school, we have all come across the student who is above and beyond. These students often excel beyond the level of their peers because they are especially gifted or talented, or perhaps have an enthusiasm for the subject, a thirst for knowledge, that drives them on to take their learning beyond the curriculum. Here is one approach to help these exceptional students fly.

The Accelerated Learning Contract is rooted in personalised learning and is a proactive way to cater for the most able students, instead of adopting responsive, *ad hoc* extension or enrichment opportunities. An Accelerated Learning Contract can be formed between a pupil, their teacher and parents. The purpose of the contract is to agree a plan of action for a specific period of time.

What to do

- Download an example of an Accelerated Learning Contract from the website (see Figure 5.6).

- Share with your student/s the topic areas to be covered in your scheme of learning. At this point, you should identify potential areas of extension, research and tasks that the student might want to consider, along with suitable sources of information and additional reading.

- The student then has a period of time to reflect on this work and identify their own ideas on how they would like to extend and enrich the lessons for themselves. For example, the student might want to carry out their own investigation or Independent Learning Project (page 157) to run alongside the scheme of work, which they can work on in lessons when other work has been completed. Alternatively, the student and teacher might agree a range of challenging objectives that the student can work towards in addition to those already being set.

- The purpose of the contract is not only to agree the focus of this extension and enrichment, but to agree a set of rules, such as when the student is allowed to work on their enrichment task. The signing of the Accelerated Learning Contract might take place at a formal meeting with the parents attending.

Accelerated Learning Contract	
Student:	
Subject:	
Topic area:	
Duration of learning	
Current areas of focus and content:	Proposal for extension and enrichment:
Accelerated learning objectives for extension and enrichment:	
Support and suggested sources:	
Terms and conditions:	
Students signature	
Teachers signature	
Parents signature	

Figure 5.6 Accelerated Learning Contract

Interest Inventories

Being able to adapt the learning experience to your students' interests, personalities and backgrounds is a very powerful way to personalise learning. As teachers, we are able to do this when we start to know our students, but this may take some time. Why not start the journey with a new class by carrying out an Interest Inventory?

An Interest Inventory is a simple survey of each student to identify what they like, what excites them, what they find difficult and easy and how they like to learn.

What to do

The following questions might be a useful starting point for conducting an interest survey.

- What do you like to do in your spare time?
- Do you have any hobbies?
- What do you want to become when you leave school?
- Why did you choose this subject? (if it was an option)
- What are some of your favourite topics?
- What are your (other) favourite subjects? Why?
- In lessons, what types of activities do you enjoy best?
- What do you find challenging/difficult?
- What do you find easy?
- When do you learn best?

Once you have gathered this information, you can start to plan learning activities to suit individuals. This could be as simple as using a football analogy to help a footy-mad student to understand a concept or allowing students to undertake an Independent Learning Project (ILP) (page 157) based on a topic that excites them.

Teaching tip

Keeping an Interest Inventory will support lesson planning and facilitate strategies that give students choice in the process and outcome of their learning. For example, Thoughts and Crosses (page 161) and Taking the Credit (page 159).

Challenge and support

Differentiation by choice

Differentiation by choice is not about letting students do what they want, but about providing a clear structure with boundaries and rules. The following ideas help teachers provide a framework that, whilst giving students the flexibility to make their own choices and move at their own pace, ensures they are doing the right sorts of things.

Going SOLO with Baseball

The Structure of Observed Learning Outcomes (SOLO) Taxonomy was first proposed by Biggs and Collis (1982) and, over the past few years, has grown in popularity as a model applied to student learning and progression through several levels of understanding. The key benefit of this taxonomy is that it provides a system, and with it a language, that students can use to check and assess their own level of understanding on a given topic. Furthermore, the taxonomy can be used as a structure to design activities and opportunities for independent learning. Here is how I have used the taxonomy to set up 'Baseball Lessons'.

In a Baseball Lesson, students progress through four bases (or stages) with activities designed to support learning at various levels of the SOLO Taxonomy. These activities can run over several lessons and start with the teacher 'pitching' the topic at the start of the first lesson. Students start on the first base and progress at their own pace to the 'home base', where they will complete an open-ended activity of their choice. At each base, appropriate activities are used to encourage progress through the taxonomy.

What to do

- Base 1 – the first base is akin to the pre-structural or unistructural stage of the taxonomy. The purpose of the first base is for students to grasp a basic understanding of the topic or concept. Another way to look at the first base is to consider it to be the information-gathering stage. When students are at this base, it might be appropriate for the teacher to give a short input on the topic, perhaps a demonstration. This could even involve a short video prepared by the teacher or one collected from a suitable source. The benefit of using a video is that students can return to it later to recap and check their understanding while the teacher circulates and supports the other bases. Other activities that might be useful at this information-gathering base, if students are required to read extended text, are Text Trivia (page 89), Comprehension Cranium (page 88) and Ten-word Challenge (page 91).

155

- Base 2 – at the second base, teachers should aim to build students' understanding of the topic so that they are able to explain several elements or issues. This is known as the multistructural stage, where students have several ideas about the topic and will start to piece them together. At this point, there will be gaps in students' understanding so the best approach is to use collaborative activities that get students working together to fill these gaps. Some activities appropriate to this base might include Quiz Quiz Trade (page 128), Expert Groups (page 123) or Diamond 9s (page 76).

- Base 3 – the third base represents the relational stage of the taxonomy. At this level, we expect students to piece ideas together by combining what they know and appreciating how different aspects fit together. This could involve recognising the relationship between what they learnt at Base 2, or even an appreciation of how the topic fits in with other areas of the syllabus or subject. Students should now start to use what they have learnt to answer questions independently by using, for example, Thoughts and Crosses (page 161). Another good activity that will get students thinking about the connections between the parts of their understanding is Hexagonal Learning (page 57). Prepare the activity by writing key words/topics onto the hexagons, or get students to do this themselves.

- Base 4 (home base) – at the extended abstract stage, students are expected to be able to transfer the principles they have learnt to a new context; in effect, applying what they have learnt. The best way for students to do this is to solve a problem. This could be a multi-stage problem, mini project or a question that requires students to draw on their newly acquired knowledge. Hexagonal learning in a broader context could also be used at this stage, but Bloom's Challenge Wall (page 147) could also be used to give students free choice to create something unique. Students who are comfortable operating at this base could also help to support students at the other bases by using them as Student Tutors (page 125).

Overall, the transition from one base to another might come when a student has completed a set of pre-designed activities, such as those mentioned above, or perhaps by completing a hinge question (page 182) related to that level of understanding. For example, at Base 1, a hinge question might be to describe, outline or even list factors about X; whereas, at Base 3, a hinge question might encourage students to compare and contrast X with Y. Finally, at Base 4, students might be expected to evaluate the significance of X. The principles of this approach are based on designing activities to develop students' knowledge at each stage and then giving them the autonomy to move on when they are ready.

Independent Learning Projects

An Independent Learning Project (ILP) is another alternative to the traditional approach to homework. An Independent Learning Project requires students to identify their own area of interest within a topic or unit of work, and then choose a focus to investigate and create a project on. The focus of the project can be anything that the student enjoyed and found interesting. At the end of the unit of work, students will then present their projects in a final ILP lesson. This ILP lesson might take place at some point during the consecutive unit of work, to ensure students have had chance to experience all of the topics and have enough time to complete the project. The only rule for an ILP is that students have to explore a topic or concept deeper and learn something new – it cannot be based on the learning that has already taken place. Students are allowed to complete their project any way they like – for example, making a video or a model, carrying out a demonstration or writing a story.

What to do

- Launch the ILP following a unit of work, but allow students 3–6 weeks to complete it and set a date for the presentations. These will usually need to take place over a number of lessons.

- Set clear rules for the ILP to ensure students understand what is expected of them. Some useful principles to share might be:

  o engage – choose something that interests you;

  o plan – plan your project, and talk to your teacher and parents to ensure your idea will make an effective ILP;

  o investigate – explore and research your topic to find out new things;

  o create – produce something that demonstrates what you have learnt;

  o exhibit – share what you have done and learnt.

- If you intend to formally assess their projects, ensure your students understand how they will be marked and what you expect from a good example.

Students can produce some truly fantastic projects when they have permission and free rein to explore a topic that engages them. The added bonus of an ILP is that each project can enrich the learning of the whole class when new knowledge and findings are shared. The ILP lesson can be run as individual presentations or even exhibitions where other classes, and perhaps parents, are invited to attend.

Lessons that Flow

When lessons are truly differentiated, we often see different students doing different things at different times. This, of course, is easier said than done and conjures the image of the circus performer spinning multiple plates on the end of poles – a challenging, and certainly exhausting, task for any teacher.

In order to manage these multiple paths through a lesson, you can use lesson flow charts to visualise the journey a student might take through your lesson. Figure 5.7 shows an example of a flow chart I have used in a Year 7 Maths lesson.

The purpose of the flow chart is to encourage students to make their own decisions about when to move on to a new topic or the next challenge. The square nodes in the diagram indicate the main activities I expect students to work on during the lesson. As students feel confident in their understanding, they can give themselves the 'green light' to move on to the next task. The diamond node represents a live demo I might give the class or an explanation of a concept. The

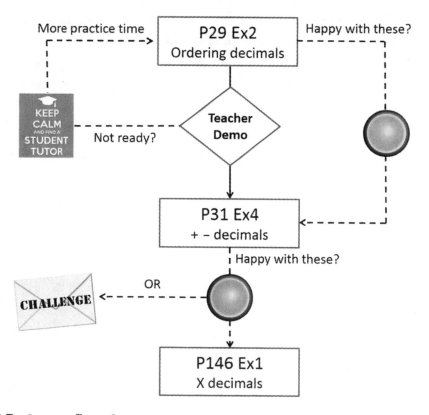

Figure 5.7 Lesson flow chart

students who don't require this support can naturally move on to the next activity. The flow chart also encourages students to work together if they need more help – for example, using Student Tutors (page 125) – and towards the end of the lesson students have a choice in the extension activity they complete (Challenge Envelope, page 150).

The lesson flow chart is a useful tool as it gives students a visual set of instructions to follow, encourages progress and provides an element of choice. Not to mention the benefits to the teacher of not having to constantly repeat a set of instructions. It also shows the class that it is fine for students to be at different stages during a lesson and highlights the opportunities for support and extension.

What to do

- Start your flow chart by adding the key activities you plan to use during the lesson.

- Once you have done this, add any points where you plan to bring the class together to give instructions or a demonstration. These can be compulsory or optional for those students who need extra support.

- Finally, add additional extension activities and sources of support that students can use throughout the lesson.

Teacher tip

It is sometimes useful to add times to the flow chart – for example, to represent the stage you expect most students to reach by a certain point in the lesson, or the time you will gather a group of students together for a discussion.

Taking the Credit

An alternative to setting fixed tasks for homework is to provide students with choice through a credits system. This system can be used over a period of time, perhaps a topic or unit of work. The point is to offer students a range of activities linked to relevant content. Each piece of work is assigned a number of credits based on the complexity and time demands. Students then choose a range of activities to achieve a set points total (e.g. 50 credits).

The point of the credits system is to give all pupils the opportunity to present their learning in their own way and to get them thinking about how they learn. Table 5.1 shows an example of a homework credit system related to a Key Stage 3 Religious Studies unit of work on being reflective and self-critical.

Table 5.1 Homework credit system

Piece of work	Number of credits
Menu for a Rosh Hashanah meal	10
Bake a Rosh Hashanah cake and write up the experience	10
Research the origins of the Jewish Calendar	10
Research on Janus and its association to new year	10
Interview three people about their thoughts on Yom Kippur	15
Meditation diary	20
Diary account for a nun attending a Pavarana day	15
A piece of art work that is related to being reflective and self-critical	20
A poem about being reflective	15

What to do

- Decide on a credit scoring system to use with the homework.

- Decide on a variety of creative tasks for students to choose from. Make sure there is sufficient variety to cover different learning styles and approaches (perhaps look back over you Interest Inventory to get ideas on the sorts of things that interest your students).

- Allocate points to each task based on complexity and the time it will take to complete.

- Discuss each piece of homework with your class so that they understand your expectations. Finally, set a deadline for all tasks to be completed.

Teaching tip

Although it is not necessary to set students deadlines for specific pieces of work, it is important that students hand their homework in on a regular basis to ensure you have time to mark it. You don't want everything being handed in at once.

Targeted Objectives

Targeted Objectives are effective when building a lesson around tiered learning. Bronze, silver and gold learning objectives (see Figure 5.8) are shared with students at the start of a lesson. Each level can contain multiple objectives and intended outcomes. Students then choose the objective, or set of objectives, for which they will be aiming. These objectives can be linked to level criteria and, therefore, this guides students to the most appropriate objectives for their target level. As students achieve bronze and silver objectives, they can be encouraged to move on to silver or gold. This approach to lesson objectives can also be used alongside a rewards system.

What to do

- At the start of a lesson, students will consider and choose a level they are aiming for and indicate this to the teacher (perhaps using a mini whiteboard).

- During the course of the lesson, the teacher can then challenge those students who they feel should be targeted at a higher level. Students should be able, and actively encouraged, to raise their targets at any point.

Thoughts and Crosses (or Tic-tac-toe)

In order to add variety to a project or set of homework, use a tic-tac-toe grid to offer students an aspect of choice. Students have to choose a row, column or diagonal of three pieces of work they will complete for the project. Students may choose activities which best suit their learning style or interest, but a carefully constructed grid ensures that all students complete certain types of tasks. For example, placing a written task in the three squares that make up either diagonal line will ensure each student has at least one piece of written work for the teacher to assess.

Variations

Other uses of the tic-tac-toe approach might include:

- choosing three words or techniques to use in a piece of creative writing;

- choosing three numbers to solve a calculation (like Countdown);

- choosing three topics to talk about for an oral assessment;

	Bronze Objectives
	Silver Objectives
	Gold Objectives

Figure 5.8 Targeted Objectives

- choosing three acting techniques to include in a piece of drama;

- choosing three question stems to form their own questions.

Tic-tac-toe can be applied to any subject with a bit of imagination and, of course, you can fill the grid with nine questions to let pairs compete against one another – 'Thoughts and Crosses'. First student to get three correct answers in a line wins!

Ten Minute Taste for Teaching

With a bit of forward planning and preparation, it is possible to involve the whole class in sharing the responsibility of teaching by getting them to prepare an introduction to a new topic and engage the audience in an activity, possibly one that tests their prior knowledge or assumptions. Using students to introduce a topic is a great way to create class experts and it also makes introductions to new topics more memorable as students will pay extra attention when it is one of their peers teaching the class.

What to do

- Before the start of a new topic or scheme of learning, allocate discrete topics to individuals or pairs. I have always allocated topics randomly by getting students to draw lots.

- Students are then required to prepare a ten-minute introduction on their allotted topic at the start of a pre-scheduled lesson. The key is to give students plenty of notice and time to research and prepare. I usually spend five minutes with each individual or pair to ensure they have a clear understanding of what I am expecting and they know where to access the relevant information.

- Encourage students to include activities and involve the audience, as this takes a bit of pressure off them to present for a full ten minutes and makes for a more engaging starter. One option is to give students a menu of activities to choose from, such as a range of starters.

- When all of the topics have been distributed, produce a schedule with dates and hand it out so that everyone knows when they will be presenting. It is also a good idea to give your class regular reminders about upcoming introductions, so you don't get a panicked expression when you ask a student to join you at the front of the class when they've forgotten to prepare.

Teaching tip

Get your students to submit their proposals via email so you can check that the main points are being covered. If necessary, you can then have a quick chat with any students who need a bit of support and guidance. Students will only be covering the basic points of a topic, but you want to make sure they are on the right lines.

Works well with

- Ten Minutes of TED (page 100).

Questioning to stretch and challenge

The use of good questioning is covered in several chapters of this book. However, the ideas in this section are particularly aimed at encouraging students to think harder, take responsibility and improve the quality of the answers they give.

A Token Question

Part of challenging students is to ensure they think for themselves, instead of asking the teacher for constant support and instruction. One way to ensure students are more efficient and cautious with their questions is to assign students with question tokens (Figure 5.9). These are then exchanged for an answer when your students ask questions.

What to do

- Each lesson students are assigned a number of tokens (decided by the teacher and dependent on the context of the class).

- Each time a student asks the teacher a question, they must hand over one of their tokens in return for an answer. Students cannot ask a question unless they have a token to trade. This will ensure students think carefully about each question before they ask it and, hopefully, attempt to answer questions themselves to save their tokens.

- Students can also use the tokens as a currency in exchange for useful/correct answers. In order to avoid situations where students run out of tokens but really need support from the teacher, offer a buyback option where students can redeem a token for answering several other questions posed by the teacher.

Figure 5.9 Question token

Variations

Tokens can also be used to encourage participation. At the start of a group exercise, distribute an even number of tokens to each student. Whenever they make a contribution or idea to the group, they can then place one of their tokens in the centre of the table. The aim is for each student to use all of their tokens by the end of the task, hence ensuring that every student has an equal contribution to the activity. This works in a similar way to the group work pie chart discussed on page 72.

Solve It

It is important to foster a culture of independence in your classroom and part of this involves coaching students to solve problem for themselves, rather than going straight to the teacher at the first sign of a challenge. There are a number of useful acronyms/phrases that a teacher can adopt, and perhaps display, in their classrooms to remind students of the steps they should take to get them unstuck. Here are a few:

- 3B4ME – students use three alternative sources before asking the teacher for help;

- Brain, Book, Buddy, Boss – a little more prescriptive and encourages the student to persevere and give adequate thinking time (brain) before seeking additional support;

- The third, and probably favourite for the students – SNOT (self, neighbour, other, teacher).

All are great tools and easy to implement in the classroom. Whenever students 'get stuck', it is important for them to stay stuck for a while. By this I don't mean that they should sit there twiddling their thumbs or turning round to distract a friend, but they should be encouraged to think a little longer, reread the question and try to solve the problem for themselves. Figure 5.10 shows another model that students can adopt to help them manage problems before seeking support from someone else. There are five steps to the 'Solve It' model.

What to do

- Step 1 – whenever a student proclaims to be 'stuck' or tells you they 'don't get it', your first response should be, 'Why are you stuck?' For some, this is quite a baffling question, but the purpose is to help them focus their attention on the cause. The actual barrier could be they did not understand the instructions, a key term that baffles them or, the most annoying barrier of all, they've not even read the question! If students ask themselves this question before putting their hand up for help, it can sometimes be a sufficient remedy in itself.

- Step 2 – ask students to 'chunk it' and break the problem down into more manageable tasks.

- Step 3 – encourage students to use any other resource to which they have access to 'find it' (the answer), including the Internet, a textbook or their own notes.

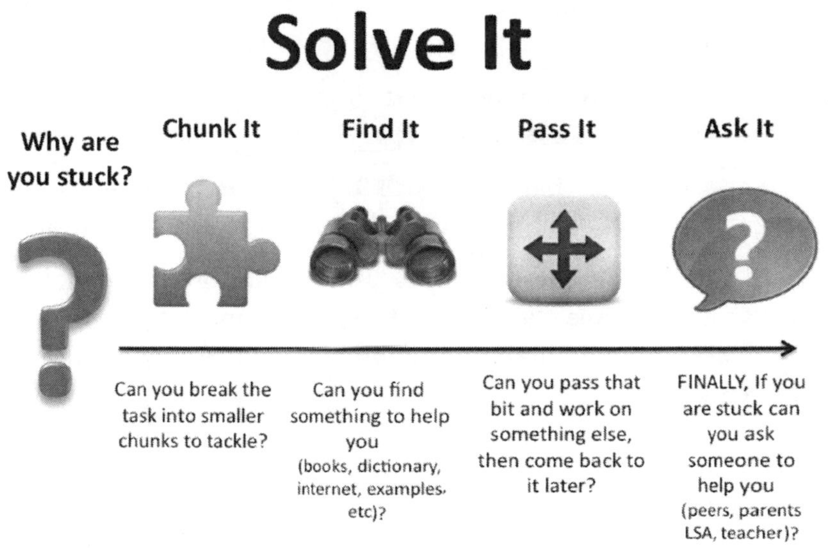

Solve It

Why are you stuck?	Chunk It	Find It	Pass It	Ask It

Can you break the task into smaller chunks to tackle?	Can you find something to help you (books, dictionary, internet, examples, etc)?	Can you pass that bit and work on something else, then come back to it later?	FINALLY, If you are stuck can you ask someone to help you (peers, parents LSA, teacher)?

Figure 5.10   Solve It

- Steps 4 and 5 – these might happen simultaneously, as it is not always pos-sible for a student to receive immediate support from a teacher or friend if they are otherwise engaged. Therefore, a student might decide to 'pass it' if 'ask it' is not an option. Displaying a Solve It poster in your classroom, or any of the other tools, is an effective way to remind students to take responsibility for their own learning and not to give up.

Questions that FLOW

Here is one model of direct questioning that will help you to assess the under-standing of a range of students, involve the whole class and facilitate higher-order thinking. The FLOW model helps teachers to build a string of questions from a basic factual or knowledge question, with each subsequent question involv-ing new students and becoming more challenging. The FLOW model is effective when used to direct questions as it demands every student to be actively listen-ing and thinking. This is because each subsequent question is based on the pre-vious answer. The FLOW model has four stages, as the acronym suggests, and might be used to engage at least four students from one opening question. This approach naturally takes the line of questioning through Bloom's Taxonomy.

What to do

- Ask a factual question that elicits a factual descriptive or simple explana-tion from a student.

- Ask a second student (or stick with the first student) to develop the answer with further detail or an appropriate example.

- A third student can now be asked to give their opinion on the first two answers. This could be an alternative approach or asking if they agree.

- The final stage of the chain is to ask a fourth student (or one of the first three) any sort of question that begins with why, where, which, how or what if.

- As each subsequent question in the chain builds on the previous answer, it means that the whole class has to be engaged and listening. A summary of this process is shown in Table 5.2, with an example conversation outlined in Figure 5.11.

Making a Statement

The most common way to differentiate questioning as a written task is to use grad-ually more challenging questions. These will often tie in with Bloom's Taxonomy and start with some basic factual or descriptive responses, and move on to more

Table 5.2 Summary of Questions that FLOW

Fact: factual question	What is. . .? Give me an example of. . .? Who did. . .?
Link: linked strand of development	Tell me more. . . What do you mean by. . .? Can you explain it?
Other: options/ideas	Give me another example? Is there another way? Do you agree?
Which (or any other 'W')	Which is the best? What if? Why did he/she say that?

challenging evaluative ones. However, using a tiered approach to questioning in this manner can exclude some students from the most difficult questions and create unnecessary work for the most able. One alternative approach to asking a gradation of questions is to use statements – for example, 'All countries should invest more in renewable forms of energy' or 'Lennie is the least dynamic character in Steinbeck's novel *Of Mice and Men*'. Both of these statements are opinions that form an open question. All that is required is to ask students to respond to these statements. For some, answering this type of question requires a little practice because there is no direction, but, in effect, all students should be able to comment on these statements with a bit of guidance, depending on their level of understanding. For example, in the first statement, some students will be able to give examples of renewable energy and perhaps cite the benefits. Other students may be able to provide a counterargument to renewable sources, a limitation, or maybe their own evaluation. The great thing about using statements in a lesson is that all students will be able to access them at different levels. Statements are a great way to formatively assess students and can form the basis of a lesson. When using the lesson planning structure outlined in Chapter 1, it is also useful to make note of any assessment statements you intend to use during the lesson using the formative assessment box on the lesson plan template (Figure 1.1).

Top ten strategies to support students

In this chapter, we have discussed a range of strategies that can add more challenge to your lessons. Here are some simple ideas that can give students a bit more support when they need it.

1. Word Banks

When students are faced with learning a wide range of technical terminology, it might be useful to adopt Word Banks. A Word Bank is not simply a glossary of key terms, but a collection of synonyms that students can use to apply more advanced terminology in their work (for example, see Table 5.3). Word Banks

Student 1 – Factual question

Teacher: Immie, what is a franchise?

Immie: It's a business that licenses its products so other people can set up a business to sell them ... a bit like copying a business.

Teacher: Thanks, Immie.

↓

Student 2 – Linking/developing question

Teacher: Wayne, what are the benefits of setting up as a franchise for a franchisee?

Wayne: The franchisor helps you.

Teacher: How?

Wayne: They might give you some training and you get their recognised brand image.

Teacher: Excellent!

↓

Student 3 – Other/alternatives question

Teacher: Sidrah, are there any alternatives to setting up a franchise?

Sidrah: Yeah, you could set up as a sole trader.

Teacher: Which is?

Sidrah: A business owned by an individual with unlimited liability.

Teacher: Well done, Sidrah. I'm pleased you mentioned limited liability.

↓

Student 4 – Which/What if question

Teacher: And Liam, which would you say is the best type of setup – Franchise or Sole Trader?

Liam: Erm.. probably a franchise because it can be safer and lots of the hard work is done for you. You're not starting from scratch.

Teacher: Well done, Liam – that was a good answer.

Figure 5.11　Example of Questions that FLOW

can also be used to help students understand complex vocabulary by replacing them with simpler terms or phrases. Blank Word Banks can be given out at the start of a topic so students can complete them over a series of lessons. Teachers can offer alternative phrases as new vocabulary is introduced.

2. Half-finished Notes

To aid students who find it challenging to produce their own set of notes during a lesson, provide half-finished notes. Half-finished notes could include word fills, partially completed diagrams, sentence starters or writing frames.

3. Picture Clues

This is a simple approach that can be applied to notes and slideshows to help students decipher words and memorise their meaning. If you are an artistic type (or even if you're not), students will appreciate your doodles to help them learn. Take, for example, this Biology Picture Clue for 'hormone' (Figure 5.12) – *a chemical message carried around the body in the blood to the organs that they affect.*

4. Engaging Learning Styles

Tailoring a lesson to the needs of different learning styles can happen when resources and activities are presented through different media. For example,

Table 5.3   Example of a Word Bank

Advanced vocabulary		Normal vocabulary	
Mosquito	Buttresses	Insect	Large roots
Canopy	Dense	Tree tops	Crowded trees
Humid	Decomposing	Sticky	
Emergents	Carnivores	Tallest trees	
Liona	Trepidation		

Figure 5.12   'Hormone' Picture Clue

launching a task using a video or podcast rather than, or in addition to, a written page. Students can also be allowed a choice in the way they complete their work, such as creating a labelled diagram, a song or a model. We should always try to get students up and moving at least once in a lesson. Whether this is just moving seats or taking part in an activity, this will engage, or at least refresh, kinaesthetic learners. Provide an extra element of support for visual learners by incorporating a range of graphic organisers as discussed in Chapter 2 whenever possible – for example, flow charts, Venn diagrams, thinking maps, storyboards and images. Even more useful is when these diagrams are displayed around the classroom as reference material for students to access as and when they need to.

5. Talking and Thinking Before Inking

Create a routine of students talking through a learning activity before starting it. This could take the form of a 'think–pair–share' activity to encourage collaboration and support so that students are more confident putting pen to paper.

6. Chunking

To 'chunk' is to use short and concise activities with a measurable time limit (perhaps use a visual timer or stop watch). Chunking will help keep pace in a lesson and ensure students do not have to stay focused for an extended period of time. Chunks are supported by frequent progress checks to assess learning and to make progress, and therefore success, visible.

7. Live Modelling

This should not be limited to a teacher giving a demonstration – for example, solving an equation, dissecting a plant or identifying a four-figure grid reference. Live Modelling could also involve a teacher taking students through the thinking process, perhaps in the form of a monologue – speaking their thoughts aloud to demonstrate the sorts of ideas and thinking the students might go through in completing a task. Students then attempt the task immediately after watching the teacher.

8. Scaffolding

This technique can be used to prompt ideas through a writing frame. A writing frame might present students with a paragraph structure, sentence starters and useful connectives to link ideas together and develop meaning. See, for example, the AfL Dashboard (page 177), an example of which can be downloaded from the website.

9. Quick Turnaround Homework

Some students find it challenging to meet homework deadlines or complete their homework at all. A Quick Turnaround Homework could even be the next day, provided a structure is put in place to support the student. This might involve an agreement with parents or SEN support staff. It might also be useful to email these parties and inform them of the task and expectations. If your school or department offers a homework club, this is another source of support. It is important that a quick turnaround of homework is facilitated by a reward system and timely feedback to praise success.

10. EAL learners

I am going to cheat a little with this last point as there are a range of strategies that deserve mentioning that are specific to students with English as an additional language. It goes without saying that most of the strategies previously mentioned also have obvious benefits for EAL students, such as scaffolding writing tasks, Half-finished Notes and Word Banks. However, here are just a few suggestions that are specific to their learning needs.

- *Progress Not Attainment* – many EAL students will be very able, but because of language barriers will struggle on tests and examinations. In early assessments, it is likely that their results will be considerably lower than some other students and this can have a damaging effect on motivation and confidence. When students are absorbed in a new language, they will often make significant improvements in a short space of time and the focus should clearly be placed on the improvements these students have made from one assessed piece of work to the next. This is particularly important to emphasise in cultures where importance is firmly placed on top grades and high test scores.

- *Cultural Reference Buddies* – EAL students have to contend not only with a new language, but with a new culture too. Most EAL students will not appreciate the cultural background and contexts that we take for granted and one idea is to assign a 'Cultural Reference Buddy' to sit with an EAL partner to explain cultural and colloquial references made during lessons. This is a far less daunting task for a student than having to support an EAL student in other aspects of their work and it also helps integrate EAL students within your class.

- *Short Homework* – perhaps another obvious point, but EAL students will take far longer to complete a piece of homework. Set shorter tasks and ask them to keep a homework log as a record of how long each piece of work took them. Encourage them to be completely honest with their record as this can be a useful tool for you to help them manage their workload.

- *Down Time* – EAL students need to listen extremely carefully to everything that is said in order to pick out, from the jumble of words they do not know, those that they recognise and can make sense of. The normal school day will require more concentration than it does for other students and this can be extremely tiring. There may be times in a lesson when you can give them a break. Even if you are talking to other people in the class, EAL students may be trying to listen so they don't miss anything. Give them a signal that shows they can have a break and switch off. Then perhaps use another signal to indicate it is necessary for them to listen.

- *Note-taking* – encourage EAL students to take their own notes and use strategies to help them do this. As previously mentioned, provide them with Half-finished Notes that only require key vocabulary to be entered. Ensure notes and worksheets are designed with enough space so that they can add their own additions in the margins and, if possible, provide them with textbooks that they can keep and build up with their own annotations.

Chapter summary

In this chapter, we have introduced a range of strategies to help teachers challenge students and push their learning on, personalise the learning experience and support students so that they can access learning at different points. Many of these ideas can be used as 'add-ons', introduced when necessary to deal with students with particular needs, such as Secret Missions or Personalised Learning Contracts. Others are strategies that can run in the background for students to access on demand, such as Solve It or Bloom's Challenge Wall. We have also covered a range of strategies that encourage good questioning, unpick understanding and challenge assumptions. This is a theme that we will continue to explore in Chapter 6 as we discuss the use of questioning to review progress.

Although these tools are effective and have their place, the real work that goes on to differentiate learning is far more subtle and comes from the day-to-day interactions, the questions and discussions, that help us build an understanding of our students' needs and their personalities. As we do this, we start to build trusting relationships and this is the point at which learning really becomes differentiated.

Students should find challenge in every lesson and, where necessary, the right level of support to help them along. Students need the right balance of challenge and support in order to grow and make progress and it is our job as teachers to help them find a happy medium in the classroom.

6

Assessment for learning

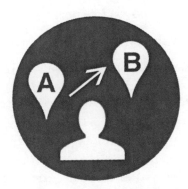

The analogy of a road map or journey is as good as any to help explain the philosophy of assessment for learning. In essence, assessment for learning means the strategies we use to help our students understand their current location as learners (their knowledge, skills and abilities), their final destination (the goals and outcomes of their learning) and the route they will take to get there (the learning activities that will help them progress). The task of helping our students get from A to B is never a straightforward process. We know there will have to be detours along the way and not every student will take the same route. It is assessment for learning that gives us the tools to shape this learning journey. Similarly, Black *et al.* (2002) define assessment for learning as 'the process of seeking and interpreting evidence for use by learners and their teachers to decide where the learners are in their learning, where they need to go and how best to get there'.

Black *et al.* (2003) outlined five key principles of assessment for learning. These have stood the test of time and are the key mechanisms we use, as teachers and students, to collect and interpret evidence to inform learning. In this final part of the book, I will outline a range of practical strategies for each:

- clarifying and sharing learning intentions and criteria for success;

- engineering effective classroom discussions, questions and learning tasks;

173

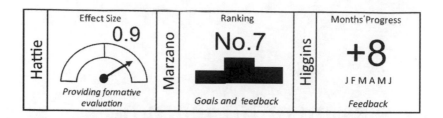

Figure 6.1 Evidence-based research acknowledges the importance of assessment for learning; most notably the value of formative feedback and target setting on student achievement.

- providing feedback that moves learners forward;
- activating students as the owners of their own learning;
- activating students as instructional resources for one another.

I decided to make assessment for learning the last section of this book, not because it is the least important; on the contrary, I felt it had to come last because it draws on everything that has preceded it. It underpins every aspect of effective teaching and learning.

Assessment for learning is the most accurate tool we have at our disposal to effectively plan effective lessons. To flog our previous analogy a little more, assessment for learning provides a satnav for each and every lesson so that we can stay on course, whilst at the same time learning how to learn. When students are accountable for their own learning and the formative assessment process, they become actively engaged – learning is not just something that is happening to them; they are responsible for it. The only way to activate students as resources for their own and each other's learning is to encourage collaborative techniques, and if assessment for learning is about shaping the learning experience to meet the needs of each student, then by definition it is fundamental to differentiated learning.

As we can see, assessment for learning is at the heart of good teaching and learning and that is why it is so important for helping students make progress towards their potential.

Sharing learning expectations and modelling good practice

Sharing learning expectations goes beyond telling students what their learning objectives are. It is about giving learners the information to make judgements about their own work and help them make informed decisions about the design, detail and structure of their next piece of work. My first headteacher, Alan Kelly, referred to this as 'making sure they know the rules of the game'.

Checklists

This is perhaps an obvious way to provide guidance on success criteria, but checklists can be used to help students understand what we are looking for and help them assess their own progress, as they go along. Checklists are particularly effective when devised with your students as this encourages buy-in.

What to do

- Your first task is to decide whether you want to hand students a checklist or involve them in forming it. If you have the time, it is always better to let your students lead on this as you can always throw in a couple of your own criteria should they miss anything out.

- It also helps to provide a level of gradation to a checklist. Ask your students to explain what the best piece of work would look like and then pick out the most tangible points and add them to the checklist. You can then ask the same questions of what a 'good' piece of work would look like and, then, what a poor piece would consist of. You can throw a couple of common mistakes into the 'poor' category too.

- Once the three levels have been clarified, your students have not only a checklist for what they need to do, but a way of measuring the quality of their own work.

- Before students complete the work, or hand it in if it is a piece of homework, ask them to identify which category they would put it in – 'poor',' good' or 'best'.

Variations

Modelling homework – instead of spending a considerable amount of time explaining how students can improve, photocopy an excellent example from one student and return it with each piece of homework. This exemplar can then be used as a reference point to highlight best practice and to demonstrate particular skills. This saves time explaining 'what you were looking for' and at the same time gives status to the exemplary student. This works well when you can rotate the exemplar to different students each week.

Bad Answers

Showing students a good example is a really effective way to help them understand what you are looking for. However, showing students a bad example can be just as effective. Indeed, no matter what subject you teach, there is always a collection of common mistakes, those bugbears that students typically get wrong time after time. A 'Bad Answer' is one way to highlight these mistakes so that your students avoid making them.

What to do

- Create your own bad example of a piece of work. This could be your own creation or simply a collection of mistakes recently made by your students.

- Hand the 'Bad Answer' out or return it with a set of homework and get your class to annotate bad practice and/or provide feedback with comments.

- They will enjoy criticising the work if you produced it, whilst at the same time learning to understand the common mistakes that people make.

Gismos for teachers on the go

Visualisers

Visualisers are a great way of sharing good examples of work as they happen during a lesson. It is sometimes easier to share examples of students' work in practical or performance-based subjects, but anything written down on paper is often difficult to share with the whole class at once. The opportunity to capture exemplary work in the spur of the moment has traditionally been the dispensation of those fortunate enough to have one of these sought-after devices in their classroom. Or at least those teachers with enough foresight to book the privileged piece of equipment if they share one in a department and it happens to be free. Visualisers are a great way to share learning expectations and model good practice, but unfortunately entry-level prices starting at £110+ make them a luxury. In most IT suites, and with the advent of tablet computing, it is now easy to grab your student's screen and project it onto the teacher's board or across every other screen, but we are not quite at the point where tablets in every classroom are commonplace. Getting students to highlight key exam skills, give live demonstrations or share a WAGOLL (what a good one looks like) is a great way of learning, and effective IT solutions can make this quick and simple. A flexible neck (also known as 'gooseneck') USB webcam with a built-in light is a far cheaper alternative (around £20) to an expensive piece of kit that you can plug into your laptop and store in your bag or top drawer.

Talking Tins

These were originally designed to help people with sight loss but are a popular tool in primary schools as a device for students to leave messages for one another or for a teacher to provide personalised instructions. These handy

Figure 6.2   USB visualiser and Talking Tin

palm-sized discs come in two variations with recording times of 20 or 40 seconds via a single button (www.talkingproducts.com). Recording a short message can be an effective strategy to support students with additional guidance. Placing one or more Talking Tins around the room (they also stick to the whiteboard!) is one way to provide a unique set of instructions to help a group or an individual without having to neglect other learners. Talking Tins can be used to remind students of the success criteria, differentiate activities and deliver extension tasks. Students will enjoy listening to their personalised message as they make progress at their own pace.

Works well with

- Challenge Envelope (page 150)
- Secret Mission (page 151).

AfL Dashboard

A dashboard is a user interface that works as a management information tool and is used to display information, often graphically, on a single page or screen. The dashboard therefore presents the user with everything they need to know to make important decisions. We can use this approach to share key exam information and success criteria with students during lessons. An AfL Dashboard is a laminated A3 information sheet that students use as a placemat. An AfL Dashboard puts key information at the fingertips, making it accessible whenever students need it.

What to do

- Download an example of an AfL Dashboard from the website.
- The dashboard contains important information that students can access during a lesson. The first step is to decide on the information you want to include. For example:

- key exam skills;

- model writing frames;

- level descriptors;

- key vocabulary;

- assessment criteria;

- classroom rules;

- reward schemes;

- the 'big picture' of learning intentions;

- good examples.

- A well-designed dashboard will often contain lots of information so it is important that it is designed appropriately, using colour, images, diagrams and tables to make the information easy to process.

- A dashboard can also be personalised to include target grades and with space left to record achievements, results and rewards.

Thinking Hats Writing Frames

The Six Thinking Hats is a term used to describe the tool for group discussion and individual thinking developed by Edward De Bono and published in his 1985 book of the same title. The Six Thinking Hats can help students organise their discussions around a topic in a systematic way. Each coloured hat represents a different way of thinking, which can be applied to a variety of situations, such as discussing problems, generating new ideas and solutions or processing information. The technique of the Six Thinking Hats has long been used in an educational setting to good effect for structuring effective discussions; however, it can be used in other ways to model effective writing techniques.

What to do

- Before starting the activity, students must have an appreciation of each hat and the type of thinking related to each colour. You can download some useful resources from the website to help you introduce the concept.

- Before starting an extended piece of writing, get students to arrange the Thinking Hats into a writing frame. Each hat can represent a different paragraph and can be used multiple times. A set of Thinking Hat cards could be used to good effect.

- This process gets students to think about the purpose of their answer and plan the relevant components in a sensible order. For example, Figure 6.3 outlines two writing frames, each with a different purpose.

- The process of discussing the structure of an answer and representing it using the Six Thinking Hats is an effective way to model good practice.

Teaching tip

To add a bit of fun to proceedings, download the origami Thinking Hats from the website. Each colour includes a selection of questions to prompt the appropriate types of thinking required when wearing each hat.

Questioning to review progress

Throughout this book, we have explored a variety of different techniques for questioning. This has included questioning to encourage deeper thinking, questioning for collaborative enquiry and questioning to challenge students and differentiate learning. In these three instances, questioning is used not to find out what students know, but as a vehicle for further learning. However, in this section, I will look at those techniques that help us review students' progress in order to inform teaching.

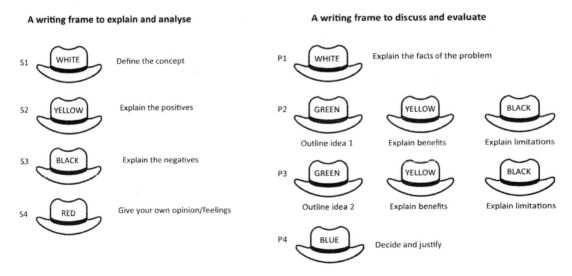

Figure 6.3 Thinking Hats Writing Frames

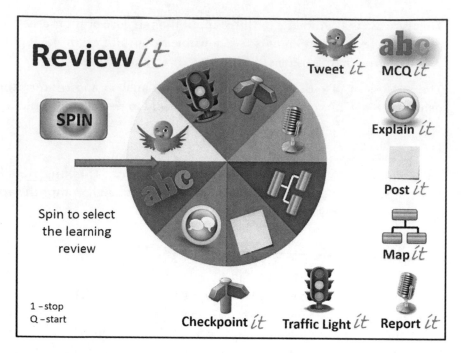

Figure 6.4   Review Wheel

The Review Wheel

The Review Wheel is an eight-segment spinner that contains eight simple techniques for reviewing learning in 2–5 minutes. The Review Wheel then acts as a simple checkpoint that can be dropped into a lesson to review progress. The Review Wheel runs as a slide in a PowerPoint presentation and randomly selects one of the eight techniques on the press of a button. The eight ideas outlined below are quick and simple to use. However, they add little if simply used to recap or summarise the work that has just taken place. The real value of reviewing the learning comes when decisions are made about the direction of learning based on the needs of your students. In effect, each of these ideas should be used to answer the question 'Where do we go from here?'

What to do

- Download the Review Wheel from the website or create your own using the template.

- When ready to carry out a review, run the PowerPoint and ask a student to tell you when to stop the spinner. Selecting the image where the spinner stops will then take you to the relevant instructions slide. Alternatively, choose a review yourself that suits your lesson.

- *Traffic Light It* – using a class set of red, amber and green cards is one of the easiest ways to quickly check students' confidence levels. Simply highlight the lesson objective or criteria and ask each student to show the card that corresponds to their assessment of their own understanding. The limitation of this approach, and other similar techniques such as thumbs up/down, is that there is no real check involved. A student may hold up a green card just to avoid any attention. Nevertheless, this type of review is useful when grouping students for the next activity. For example, 'greens' might push on to a new task, 'ambers' might do some work together to consolidate what they have leant, whilst the 'reds' might gather around the teacher to look at the topic from a different perspective.

- *Tweet It* – in no more than a tweet, get your class to write a statement that summarises what they have learnt. Condensing what you have learnt can be a tricky task. Get your students to read out their tweets when they have composed them and, of course, there is nothing stopping them from tweeting it for real.

- *MCQ It* – students have to create a multiple-choice question based on an aspect of their learning from the lesson. A good multiple-choice question can be difficult to write and coming up with suitable 'distracters' requires students to think deeper about the topic they are studying.

- *Explain It* – students work in pairs for 2–3 minutes and take it in turns to explain to each other what they have learnt so far. This approach encourages students to bring up areas of disagreement or misunderstanding. As pairs discuss what they have learnt, circulate the classroom and listen in to the conversations in order to inform your next steps.

- *Post It* – give each student a post-it note and ask them to write down one thing they have learnt and a question about the topic. This could be something they are unsure of or just something they would like to discuss that relates to what they have been doing. Students then stick their post-its onto the wall. The teacher can then check the board throughout the lesson and respond accordingly to address any areas students are struggling with or build in provisions for any inquisitive questions the class may have.

- *Map It* – ask your students to use any form of graphic organiser to summarise their learning. This is a great opportunity to use Thinking Maps or any of the other approaches outlined on page 68.

- *Report It* – students are given five minutes to write a short news report explaining the learning that has taken place in today's lesson. The report could start 'Today in Mr Redfern's lesson. . .'. It works well if you are able to pass around a fake microphone!

- *Checkpoint It* – the checkpoint involves answering three simple questions: What do you know? What are you unsure of? What are we yet to find out? This approach is useful because the final question gets students to think about the bigger picture – where do we go from here?

Variations

The original Review Wheel features eight techniques, but why not come up with your own collection of reviews to suit your context and subject? The Review Wheel and templates can be downloaded from the website along with other variations featuring different techniques. See, for example, the Mathematics Review Wheel.

Hinge Questions

As mentioned, the key to using any of the strategies outlined in the Review Wheel is that they should inform the direction of the lesson after the review. Questions of this nature are referred to as 'Hinge Questions' or 'Hinge Points'. A Hinge Question is based on one important concept in a lesson that is critical for students to understand before you move on in that lesson. The lesson should be planned to go one of two or more ways depending on student understanding, as revealed in their answers to the Hinge Question. A Hinge Question can take any format as long as:

- it takes no longer than 30–60 seconds to ask or present;

- it takes no longer than two minutes for students to respond to;

- all students can respond to it simultaneously, e.g. using mini whiteboards or A, B, C, D cards to hold up;

- you can assess the responses in less than 30 seconds;

- the correct answer is interpretable (the correct answer can be correct only for the right reasons).

Multiple-choice or short response answers make for the best Hinge Questions.

Hinge Question example – trapeziums

Context: The lesson topic is the characteristics of trapeziums. The critical point is that students should recognise the characteristics of a trapezium. All students should respond using their mini whiteboards.

Students will be asked 'Which shape is a trapezium?' with five options students could easily guess correctly by selecting 'A' or 'D' (Figure 6.5). However,

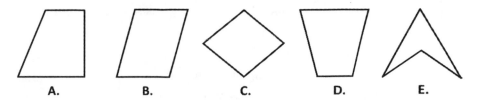

Figure 6.5 Trapezium Hinge Question

they would be unlikely to guess two answers unless they knew that A and D were both trapeziums. Using mini whiteboards means that all students can respond and the teacher can easily assess who understands the concept. Following on from this hinge point, I might ask those students who answered incorrectly to complete a short activity counting parallel lines in different shapes and then gather them together for a quick discussion of their findings, whilst those who know the distinction would move on to a new concept.

Teaching tip

If you are not comfortable with different groups of students taking different routes, you might adopt the 80/20 rule – if more than 80 per cent of students succeed on the Hinge Question, move on; anything less, time for a recap.

Works well with

- Lessons that Flow (page 158)
- Going SOLO (page 155).

Questions under the Chair

One of the best ways to engage students with questions is to get your students to ask the questions themselves. This is a nice activity that works as a starter and that can be returned to throughout the lesson and used as the plenary. Questions under the Chair can start with any sort of stimulus material, such as a newspaper article or a short video clip, but works particularly well with a picture wall or a single image. This approach also adds a bit of mystery to your lesson as students attempt to work out the topic and purpose of the lesson.

What to do

- Select an appropriate stimulus for your lesson, such as a picture, and ask your students to write down any questions that they would like answering.

The Five Ws are always a good place to start – What? Who? Where? When? Why?

- Students should write down their questions on a mini whiteboard or a post-it note and put them somewhere out of sight – under their chair.

- At the end of the lesson or a point of review, students take the questions from under their chair and see how many of them they can now answer.

- Based on the activities and learning that has taken place, students might now have some new questions that they want to add to their whiteboards or post-it notes.

Variations

Even if you don't intend to use the 'under the chair' approach, using the Five Ws and a stimulus picture, by itself, is a really effective starter activity to recap prior learning or assess the starting point for your class.

PQA (Picture, Question, Answer)

As with Questions under the Chair, this is an excellent way to introduce a topic and then review your students' progress at the end of the lesson. The activity involves students using a prompt (picture) to form their own questions around what they want to find out and then test their knowledge at the end of the lesson.

What to do

- At the start of the lesson, students are given a picture relating to the topic they are about to learn. This can be done as an individual exercise or working in pairs.

- You can be quite flexible with the pictures. The activity works just as well if all students have the same picture or a variety of pictures are distributed.

- Students are given five minutes to come up with a range of questions based on what they want to know about the picture. From the various activities during the lesson, students will gain the knowledge and understanding to answer their questions. Encouraging inquisitive minds is extremely important and it should not matter too much if some of these questions do not fit in with your learning objectives.

- During the plenary, students return to their pictures and attempt to answer their questions. The final Q&A session led by the teacher can be used to cover any additional questions.

Teaching tip

At the start of the lesson, it might be useful to remind students of appropriate questioning stems using the Question Matrix (page 55). If you run out of time and are unable to cover all of the questions during your lesson, it might also be worth adopting an approach such as the Question Box (page 54).

Formative use of summative assessment

A misconception of formative assessment is that it involves frequent and ongoing assessment of students' knowledge and ability. 'Formative assessment is only formative if the information fed back to the learner is used by the learner in improving performance' (Wiliam, 2011: 120). On the other hand, summative assessment is the assessment *of* learning and is used to summarise learning at a particular point, usually at the end of a topic, scheme of learning or project. Whilst having its criticisms, summative assessment is worthwhile and necessary in an education system driven by examination performance. Apart from its obvious benefits as a practice mechanism, we all like to test ourselves against a standard. Nevertheless, summative assessment techniques lose any value if they are not used to inform learning. Therefore, it is important that we make students the winners and not victims of summative assessment. We must learn to use the summative scores and grades we collect and hoard in our mark books in order to benefit our students. I strongly believe that the most valuable lessons are those immediately before and just after a test or mock examination, and the following strategies are a few ideas on how to make formative use of this time.

Before the test

Three to Go

It is common to review and summarise learning at the end of a topic. Quite often teachers will devote a lesson to this, especially if a summative test is to take place. Sometimes these recap lessons are used to revise as a class, perhaps constructing mind maps or revision checklists, but overall this is a great time for reflection. These can be hectic lessons and quite teacher-dominated as they stand at the front of the classroom and rattle through a whole scheme of learning. Instead, allow your students to make value judgements on the three most valuable aspects they want you to cover. Allowing your class time to decide on the three topics they most want you to review before the test, 'Three to Go' is an excellent use of your time and theirs with three particular benefits:

1. Students have to self-assess and collaboratively make decisions about what they most need to recap.

2. Students will naturally discuss each topic, ask questions and fill in the gaps in their own knowledge.

3. You have more time to engage your students if you don't have to cover everything in one lesson – quality not quantity.

What to do

- Ensure your class has a summary of every topic covered in the scheme of learning. This might be a checklist or some sort of visual organiser.

- Ask students to work in mixed-ability groups to discuss the scheme of learning and identify the three topics you will review.

- By carrying out this process, all students should have created their own priority list for revision. Students could use a system for categorising their revision, such as RAG.

- Getting students to work in mixed-ability non-friendship groups works best as the higher-ability students will help fill the gaps of the lower-ability students. Furthermore, students who work together each lesson are more likely to have the same ideas and understanding, so splitting them up exposes them to other students with other ideas and ways of explaining something.

- As a class, vote for the three topics you will review. Make a note of any others that did not make the cut – if time, you can cover these in a Q&A session at the end of the lesson.

Works well with

- The Three Buckets (page 71)

- Ask the Teacher (page 135).

Pupil Principal Examiners

This second idea is intended to get your students to understand the nature and design of the examination. In itself, this is not assessment for learning, but by understanding the purpose of the test and the style of question to be used they are able to interrogate their own learning. As teachers, and for those who are also examiners, we devise assessments by identifying what it is we want to assess. What should our students know or be able to do and how can we test this? Rarely, if at all, do students think in this way. Instead, they ask us what will be on the test so that they can make sure they learn it. Giving students the task of devising the test (but not the actual one they will take) is a worthwhile activity because it makes students focus on what needs to be assessed instead of what needs to be learned. Assigning students the role of a Principal Examiner is an effective way to help them understand the examination criteria and reduces some of the fear behind the test.

What to do

- Provide your students with the information they require to write the test. This should include an overview of the topic to be assessed, examples of the types of questions that will be used, including the marks awarded, the length of the test and the total number of marks. If you want to give your students a bit more structure, you could also provide them with guidelines on the number of questions of each style they should use.

- This activity works best in small groups and is particularly effective when the test requires diagrams, tables, graphs and maps. Asking students to produce the stimulus material for an exam is a valuable process because it gets them thinking like an examiner.

- Once each group has produced their test, take it in for marking and provide constructive feedback. Your feedback will focus on the structure of the questions and the appropriateness of the stimulus material.

- Give each group a short amount of time to make any alterations before handing it back in.

- Finally, make each test paper available to the whole class as a revision resource.

Variations

If the test paper requires the use of stimulus material, another approach is to create this yourself or take it from a past paper and give it to your students without the questions attached. Students are then required to apply their knowledge of the subject and use the map, extract or case study to find the relevant links and construct appropriate questions. For example, giving students a random four-sided shape would open the opportunity to form questions on a wide range of subjects, such as angles, area or symmetry.

After the test

Summative Sound Bites

Those lessons where we hand back the test papers fill most students with dread and, for me, always construct an image of the Victorian teacher striding about the classroom, announcing the test scores of each pupil and chastising those who underperformed by throwing their book at them. These are extremely valuable lessons; they offer the greatest opportunity for reflection and self-assessment and there are more proactive ways to conduct these lessons than the teacher simply going through the test paper at the front of the class. Summative Sound Bites is one way to get your students reflecting on their performance and sharing it with others.

What to do

- Once you have marked the test papers, identify one or two questions for each student with a highlighter. This might be a question they did well on and one they could improve on. You might also provide more detailed feedback on these particular questions.

- Get each student to produce a short sound bite explaining their answer (why it is a good answer or not) and how they could improve it. This can then be shared with other students who have produced their own sound bites for different questions.

- In order to create a sound bite, students will require the mark scheme, your constructive feedback and the means to create a short sound/video recording.

- Students can easily take a snapshot of their answer and record a voiceover for their analysis. Students could use their smartphones, a tablet computer with an appropriate app, such as Educreations or Explain Everything, or a media-sharing website such as VoiceThread.

- Once created, these sound bites can be shared with the whole class as a fantastic diagnostic tool that students can use to focus on their weaker responses.

Works well with

- Silent Gallery (would require headphones) (page 127)
- Talking Tins (page 176).

Examining the Exam

Similar to Summative Sound Bites, this approach involves students reflecting on their performance and sharing it with the rest of the class through a group presentation. Each group focuses on a different section of the exam and is required to use a selection of their own answers to analyse each question.

What to do

- Split the test down into sections and allocate each part to a group of students.

- Set each group the task of giving a short presentation on their section of the test. Their presentation should make use of a selection of their own answers to explain the following:

  o What is the purpose of each question? What is it trying to assess?

  o What does a good answer look like (using examples)?

  o How could the examples used be made even better?

- Students can scan in their answers or take pictures to use in their presentation. An interactive whiteboard, a tablet device or simply a whiteboard and dry wipe pen can be used to highlight key aspects of the questions, stimulus and answers.

Teaching tip

Record each presentation as a video and share it with your class as a valuable revision aid.

Works well with

- Ten Minute Taste for Teaching (page 162)

- Composite Answers (page 125).

Five for Five

This idea could just as easily be 'Ten for Ten', or any other denomination, depending on the nature of the test and how long you want to give your students. This is a way to get your students responding to feedback on marked work or areas for improvement on a test.

What to do

- Once students have reviewed their test papers (perhaps through 'Summative Sound Bites' or 'Examining the Exam'), they should identify any areas of their test where they could pick up five more marks. This does not have to be a single question.

- Once students have chosen how they will spend their five minutes of improvement time, give them the opportunity to make the additional changes. This encourages students to think strategically about time management and the allocation of marks in an examination.

- Finish the activity by asking individuals to explain to the class what they have done to improve their score by at least five marks.

Variations

This activity can work just as well as a peer-marking exercise where students swap work and are given five minutes to make improvements. Students may not appreciate someone else other than the teacher writing on their work, so using a photocopy might work best.

Self-assessment and peer-assessment

In order for students to clearly understand assessment criteria, they must experience using it. Activating students as assessors and not simply the object of the assessment encourages collaboration and allows them to take responsibility for their own learning. If we do not teach students how to self-assess (and therefore peer-assess), we leave them guessing as to what progress looks like. Self-assessment, coupled with peer-assessment, provides significant benefits over simply teacher-led strategies. For a start, students are more likely to interrupt one another to ask questions, whereas they might not do this with the teacher. They will use and share language that works for them and may be more willing to accept criticism from their peers than from a teacher. Furthermore, as students engage in self-assessment and peer-assessment, teachers are able to circulate and facilitate learning where it is most needed. This section outlines a variety of techniques to support self-assessment and peer-assessment. The techniques are simple, but it will take time and patience to get students to a level where their own assessment is as worthwhile and as valuable as the teacher's.

Peer Marking

One of the most effective ways to encourage assessment *as* learning is to get students working in groups around a stimulus, such as another student's work, to discuss its relative merits against a set of criteria. When peer-assessment is set up effectively and students feel confident to contribute, the discussions that ensue are teaching and learning gold dust.

What to do

- Divide the pupils into small groups.

- Give each group a copy of a piece of work that can be judged against assessment criteria. Each group should have a different piece of work. This might be exemplars you have collected from a previous year.

- The task is to mark and annotate the work with reference to the criteria. The group's judgement is recorded on a separate sheet along with the reasons for their decision with reference to the criteria. The group will include feedback to the pupil about the piece of work, how well it had been done and how it could be improved.

- When the groups have completed this task, the pieces of written work, together with the comments, are passed on to another group to analyse and discuss.

- Rotate the work until the groups have analysed each piece of work or the activity loses steam.

Peer Ordering

It is interesting to explore the perceptions that students have about the quality of a piece of work. Students will often pick out the neatest and longest piece of work as being the most accomplished. This is an activity you can use to discuss these assumptions.

What to do

- As with Peer Marking, hand out several pieces of work, but this time give each group a copy of them all.

- Now get students to order the work. This can be done with success criteria or is just as valuable an exercise without this structure.

- When each group has put the work in order of the best to the worst (it should go without saying that they should not know who the work belongs to), you can then start asking questions about their choices. In particular, questions on why one piece of work is better than another. By doing this, students will be drawing out the key success criteria themselves, not just reading it from a rubric.

Variations

Another approach is to hand out the grades you awarded separately and see if your students can match them to the correct piece of work.

AfL Playing Cards

There are many ways to use a set of cards, such as playing cards, to facilitate learning. My favourite is AfL Playing Cards (I call them this, although it is not really a game) because this is a simple and flexible way to identify key exam criteria and can be used for self-assessment and peer-assessment. Figure 6.6 gives examples of cards I have created for Business Studies.

What to do

- Put your exam success criteria onto a set of cards and give each student a deck. You can give students a full deck all at once or hand them out gradually as new skills are introduced. The cards can then be used in a number of ways:

  o Before attempting a piece of work, such as an exam question, ask students to work in pairs to pick out the cards with the exam skills that they are required to demonstrate in that particular task. This is an effective planning technique that gives students a checklist to work against.

  o A second approach is to get students to select cards from their deck and turn them over when they believe they have demonstrated that skill in their work and place it at the top of their desk. Students are therefore self-assessing and informing the teacher when they have shown a particular skill. The teacher can then circulate the class and will know exactly when to check a student's work.

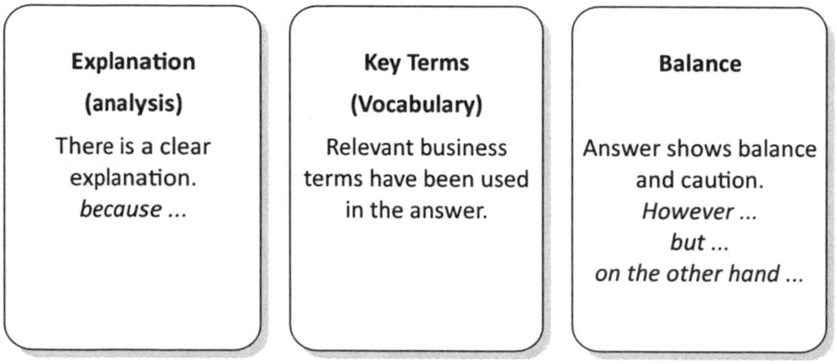

Explanation (analysis) There is a clear explanation. *because ...*	**Key Terms** (Vocabulary) Relevant business terms have been used in the answer.	**Balance** Answer shows balance and caution. *However ...* *but ...* *on the other hand ...*

Figure 6.6 AfL Playing Cards

o   A third option is to hand out an example of a piece of work and ask students to select the cards that represent the skills shown within the work. This works better than underlining or highlighting because pairs and small groups can easily compare the set of cards they selected.

RAG Reflections

This is a nice diagnostic technique that can be used to encourage peer-assessment and self-assessment after a piece of homework has been handed back to the class. It involves categorising students into three groups who will then work together to collaboratively evaluate their performance and identify areas for improvement. As you mark students' work, allocate a RAG rating to each student (a handy traffic light stamp might come in handy here). On handing the work back to students, get them to pair up into small groups as shown in Figure 6.7.

Feedback Grids

Feedback Grids are a way to get the whole class involved in peer-assessing each other's work. They require individual students to take the responsibility for giving feedback on a particular aspect of assessment as they spend a short period of time reviewing the work of their peers. The benefits of this approach are that the peer-assessment becomes easier as each student is only focusing on one aspect and every student gets detailed feedback.

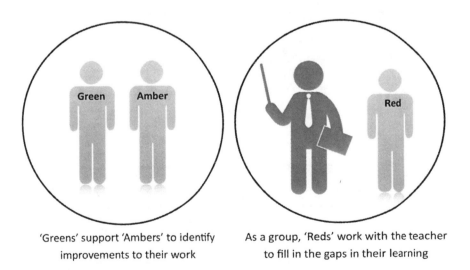

'Greens' support 'Ambers' to identify
improvements to their work

As a group, 'Reds' work with the teacher
to fill in the gaps in their learning

Figure 6.7   RAG Reflections

What to do

- Feedback Grids work best as a 'round robin' activity. Give each student a feedback frame that highlights the marking/success criteria and provides space for another student to comment on various aspects of the work (see Figure 6.8). For example, spelling, punctuation, use of examples, use of appropriate terminology, etc.

- Allocate each student a specific aspect of the work to assess and provide feedback on. This is obviously easier to do with smaller classes, but a

Peer Feedback Sheet

Name _____

Work _____

Spelling and Grammar			
(circle below)			
Excellent	Good	Needs improvement	No evidence
Comments/examples			

Context			
(circle below)			
Excellent	Good	Needs improvement	No evidence
Comments/examples			

Use of Key Terms / Technical Language			
(circle below)			
Excellent	Good	Needs improvement	No evidence
Comments/examples			

Explanation and Analysis			
(circle below)			
Excellent	Good	Needs improvement	No evidence
Comments/examples			

Evaluation			
(circle below)			
Excellent	Good	Needs improvement	No evidence
Comments/examples			

Figure 6.8   Peer Feedback Grid

large class can be broken down into two groups or you can double up on certain roles.

- The narrower the area of assessment, the easier it will be for each student to provide specific and useful feedback. As discussed, this is a skill that students develop over time – do not expect them to be experts from the outset.

- Students circulate the class reading each other's work. When they have read a piece of work, they then leave a comment in the relevant box on the Feedback Grid.

- At the end of the process, each student returns to their own work and a completed Feedback Grid containing comments on each aspect of their work.

Effective feedback through marking

All of the research suggests that feedback, boasting some of the highest effect sizes, is one of the most important factors for improving student achievement. Most teachers will be pleased to hear this, especially as so much of our time is spent marking students' work and providing them with comments on how they could do better. So, job done. Or is it? Although feedback can have a significant impact on student attainment, it comes with a caveat. Without a clear pedagogical approach to our marking of students' work, teachers may give meagre comments that, at best, provide little benefit and, at worst, send the wrong messages. Furthermore, there is also the likelihood that our students will simply ignore our feedback anyway. There is no silver bullet for effective marking. We all have to make our own decisions about what works best for us, our students and the learning in our classrooms. Nevertheless, here are my efforts at a four-step model that highlights some of the key principles that should be applied to any marking and feedback policy (Figure 6.9).

To grade, or not to grade?

Much has been debated about the impact of grading students' work, when it is not linked to GCSE or GCE external examinations. Kohn (2011) certainly provides a compelling argument. Whether it is, or is not, the best approach, here are some ideas to get the best out of any grading system you use while at the same time getting students to focus on the *why* and not just the *what*.

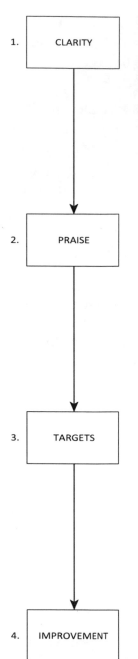

Clarity involves identifying any misconceptions that our students might have. It is not about correcting the mistakes that students make through lack of practice or carelessness. There is a range of approaches outlined in the following pages that can be used effectively to deal with this type of mistake and encourage students to self-correct. Instead, marking for clarity should demonstrate why something is correct/a good example, whilst something else is incorrect/a poor example, using statements such as 'This is what I'm looking for' or 'Can you see why this is correct and this is not?' In this way, clarity marking is a key part of sharing learning expectations and modelling success.

Dweck (2006: 75–76) highlights the dangers of praise when it is manifested in the wrong way. As she puts it, 'When you're given a positive label, you're afraid of losing it, and when you're hit with a negative label, you're afraid of deserving it.' This is why praise has to be specific and focus on effort rather than natural ability or the success itself. As highlighted through my Learning Junctions (page 61), we should praise what it takes to succeed and not the achievement itself. Menial comments like 'well done' or 'excellent work' seem to flow from our pens when we mark work; this is not necessarily a bad thing, but our comments should try to focus on the improvements and progress we see. The best praise we can give students is when we highlight not just why something is *good*, but why it is *better* than their last piece. The focus of the praise is therefore on something they have *done*, not something they *are*.

It goes without saying that one of the reasons we mark work and give feedback is to help students improve. The targets we use should also be as specific as possible. The problem with target setting is that the better the piece of work, the harder it becomes to set meaningful targets for improvement, especially when so many of our targets might refer to specific exam criteria. Therefore, how can we set meaningful targets for students who are already achieving A*? In these circumstances, it is just as useful to pose questions that make them think and question their knowledge. For example, 'Is this always the case?', 'How do you know?' or 'Is there another way?' are all good questions to ponder.

Marking and feedback is all for naught if we don't expect students to respond to our feedback and improve their work. This is why the last principle is ensuring that students take the time to respond to our feedback and make the necessary improvements. In a busy curriculum, time is precious; there are pressures to move on to the next topic, but quality time spent reflecting on work and making improvements is just as valuable as time spent on any other activity. This cycle of feedback, response and improvement creates an ongoing dialogue between teachers and students to form a record of progress and learning.

Figure 6.9   Four-part marking framework

Pre-grading

Why shouldn't our most able students be able to turn in a piece of work with their own 'pre-grade' already attached? As we train students to understand the success criteria and use grading rubrics effectively, pre-grading can get students thinking critically about their own work before they hand it in. This is most effective towards the end of a course when students have learnt and understood the examination criteria. You can then provide feedback to support or adjust the student's judgement.

Works well with

- Checklists (page 175)
- Medal and a Mission (page 198).

Delayed Grading

A graded piece of homework is always the first thing a student will look for when their work is returned and, unfortunately, too often this can distract students from the all-important feedback. Instead, record grades in your markbook and only hand students their work with clarity, praise and targets. Once students have corrected any mistakes and made improvements, then hand out the grades.

Just Comment

Why bother grading the work at all? Remove the stigma of having a grade imposed on your students by getting them to decide on the grade for themselves. This approach will demonstrate that grading is arbitrary and secondary to progress and learning. Provide your students with effective feedback that suggests how the work could be improved. Again, focus your comments on clarity, praise and targets. Get your students to work in pairs or small groups to use a grading rubric and your comments to decide on a grade for themselves.

Colourful words

A great way to emphasise key points when marking students' work is to use different colours to highlight different skills and instructions. Here are two examples:

Green Pen of Growth

Give each student a green pen. In the time you give them to read your feedback and reflect on their work, ask them to use their green pens to make the necessary corrections/improvements. Throughout their books and folders, progress will be evidenced and stand out from their original work.

Purple Pen of Progress

An aid to formative marking and useful for highlighting progress over time. Any aspect of a student's work that shows improvement from a previous piece of work could be marked, highlighted or commented on using a purple pen. Whenever students see a purple comment, they will be drawn to it as they know it is something they have shown improvement on, or perhaps a previous target they have met. Pupils will therefore associate purple ink with praise.

Framing feedback

No matter what the principles of a marking and feedback policy, it is common-place for departments to adopt frameworks to give structure and encourage consistency. Some of the most common approaches include Two Stars and a Wish, What Went Well (WWW) and Even Better If (EBI), or even simple approaches that indicate whether a piece of work is below target, on target or above target, For example, using symbols such as =, + or –.

Medal and a Mission

My favourite feedback framework is the 'Medal and a Mission'.

What to do

- Get students to take a 'Medal and a Mission' slip, like the one shown in Figure 6.10, when they have a piece of homework to complete.

- Before handing in their homework, asks students to complete the 'debrief' and attach it to their work. A 'debrief is a comment reflecting on how well they think they have performed. This could relate to the marking criteria, a checklist of good practice or highlight anything they think they have done well.

- On receiving the work, complete the 'medal' (here is where you will give your students praise) and the 'mission' (at least one target for next time or something you expect them to improve). The Medal and a Mission can be completed by the teacher or run as a peer-assessment activity.

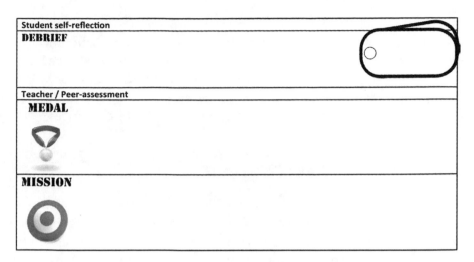

Figure 6.10   Medal and a Mission

Making improvement a priority

Signed For

Give students a table to attach to the front of their books that you can use as a checklist of work completed. Once a piece of work has been marked, the teacher writes down the title of the work, and dates and signs the checklist. Once the student has completed the corrections and improvements, they also date and sign the checklist. The next piece of work they complete will not be marked until they have made the improvements to their last piece and signed the checklist. The teacher is telling the student when and what to revise, and the student is telling the teacher when he or she is ready for the next assignment. This may seem a little draconian, but it works.

Targets at the Top (TAT)

It is frustrating when students continue to make the same mistakes, again and again. Why not adopt a system whereby students are expected to write down the target/s from their last piece of assessed work at the top of their next piece as a reminder of areas to focus on? Again, evidencing progress over time.

A Dot Marks the Spot

Small coloured sticky dots are easy to find at any stationers and act as a great way to prompt responses and improvements. Wherever you see an opportunity for a student to respond to your feedback, or make an improvement to their work, stick a dot in their book. Students should know that they have to write a response next to a dot and are not allowed to start a new piece of work directly next to/below a dot; sufficient room has to be left to give a response or make the necessary improvement. Furthermore, different coloured dots can prompt different types of responses.

Top ten marking time savers

As teachers, it sometimes feels like we 'do marking' instead of having a social life! However, when it comes to marking it is often about working smarter, rather than working harder. Here are a few strategies you can adopt to lighten the load. Let's also not forget the value of involving students in the marking and assessment process to support a culture of independent learning and self-correction.

1. Feedback Keys

To save time writing feedback on common mistakes or issues, use an abbreviated Feedback Key. This works very well when marking for literacy, but also for other issues and common types of feedback. The Feedback Key should be stuck into students' books. For example, DD = more detail and depth, Ap = application to context. The key would then go on to explain these issues and what a student might do to improve.

2. Home Peer Marking

This can work for factual or short answers and multiple-choice questions. Get students to swap homework at the start of a lesson and then give out the answers. Students will enjoy marking each other's work. Alternatively, get students to swap homework before the lesson and post the answers on the school VLE for them to access and mark prior to your next lesson.

3. Student Model Answers

Instead of spending a considerable amount of time explaining how students can improve their work, photocopy an excellent example from one student and return it with each piece of homework. This exemplar can then be used as reference to highlight best practice and to demonstrate particular skills. This saves time explaining 'what you were looking for' and at the same time gives status to the exemplary student. This works well when you can rotate the exemplar to different students each week.

4. Just Grade

Instead of providing feedback on homework or a test, simply provide a grade, but return the work with a grading rubric. Pairs or small groups then have to try to explain and justify the grade they received by highlighting key aspects of their work that match the grading criteria. This is particularly useful for helping students identify the differences between one piece of work and another.

5. One to Mark

Where there is repetition and consistency in the questions being marked (for example, several '3 markers'), then mark and provide feedback on the first couple. Allow students to have a go at marking the last question, or couple of questions, themselves using the feedback you have provided on earlier questions as guidance.

6. Focused Feedback

Get students to highlight one particular skill or aspect of their work that they would like to receive detailed feedback on – for example, spelling and grammar, technical language or appropriate connectives, or perhaps a specific skill, such as evaluation. This might work best with older and more able students who understand their own strengths and areas for development. It also helps you provide specific feedback without having to cover everything.

7. Automated Marking

Most school VLEs now have a function to produce self-marking quizzes and tests. Similarly, there are other web-based tools, such as Socrative (www.socrative.com), that can be adopted to conduct short answer or multiple-choice tests that instantly mark answers and collate the results. This will help save time on marking when assessing the knowledge-based aspects of the course.

8. Margin Marking

Comment not correct, especially when marking for literacy. Use abbreviations (see tip 1) in the margin of a student's work next to the relevant paragraph or line. The student's responsibility is then to find and correct the mistake. 'SP' in the margin should direct that student to find the spelling mistake themselves, look it up in a dictionary and make the correction. Don't do it for them!

9. Comment Keys

These are similar to Feedback Keys, but specific to a particular task and useful for extended writing. Students will often make similar mistakes and you will probably want to write the same comment multiple times. Instead, each time you identify an issue, type your comment into a separate document and number it. Then write the relevant number in the margin of the student's work. Do this for each issue that arises. You will find that the first couple of pieces take a while to mark, but your marking will speed up as you work your way through the pile and come across the same issues. Whenever I have used this approach, I find my feedback is more detailed and I haven't scrawled all over each student's work – which they don't like anyway.

10. Self-assessment and peer-assessment

Self-assessment and peer-assessment have featured in most of these ideas, but any scheme of work should make effective use of these two models alongside teacher assessment. To track progress, it might also be useful for students to highlight any assessed work with TA, SA or PA to indicate how work has been marked. Time invested at the start of a year to train students on how to assess and mark their own and each other's work and provide quality feedback will always be time well spent.

Chapter summary

In this book, we have explored the six key principles that underpin effective teaching and learning. These include effective planning and preparation, thinking skills, collaboration, engagement, differentiation and assessment for learning. All of these are evident in outstanding lessons where students make exceptional progress. The four pillars of assessment for learning pull these principles together in a number of ways. First, through developing thinking skills students are able to reflect and self-assess and, in doing so, understand their progress and potential over time. This self-awareness means they are more active and engaged in the subject and the process of learning itself. Consequently, if students understand 'where they're at' and 'where they've come from', they are more willing and likely to set themselves challenging targets as they will have the confidence to achieve them. Collaborative learning also goes hand in hand with assessment for learning. Students are themselves the best examples of good practice and by working together students use their peers as a benchmark for what they can achieve. Furthermore, through peer-assessment, students help each other identify gaps in their learning. Good formative assessment is about finding a blend of approaches that complements the various teaching and learning strategies we adopt in our lessons.

Final words. . .

As the cover states, this book is a guide to classroom practice, and as such should be used as a source of ideas that teachers can draw on to explore their trade and hone their skills. Take an idea, change it around, make it your own, share it with a colleague and encourage them to do the same. A catchy name doesn't make an idea a good one, so call it what you like. The only thing that matters is that it works for you and your students; education is not a 'one size fits all'.

There is lots of fantastic practice in UK schools and over the past few years I have been lucky to witness it in a range of contexts and to work with some outstanding teachers. Our goal as educators is to keep getting better by learning from one another and sharing best practice. Even if the sceptics say that they've seen it all before under a different banner, that doesn't mean it's not a worthwhile pursuit. Adaptation and incremental improvement is the process of innovation and, just like our students, we need to keep learning if we are going to keep up with the needs of the pupils who come through our doors tomorrow and the day after that.

There is enduring pressure in schools to achieve examination targets and help students get the best possible grades, whilst at the same time needing to uphold the mantra that every student should leave school with the right skills, attributes and values to take their place in society and a competitive, demanding world. Or perhaps the aim of schooling is about enjoyment, discovery, friendship and helping students understand where they're going in life? Whatever your educational philosophy, so long as we get the teaching and learning bit right, then none of these aims need be seen as mutually exclusive.

We need not compromise.

Our students are entitled to it all.

Bibliography

Bergmann, J. and Sams, A. (2012) *Flip Your Classroom: Reach Every Student in Every Class Every Day*, Washington, DC: International Society for Technology in Education.

Biggs, J. and Collis, K. (1982) *Evaluating the Quality of Learning: The SOLO Taxonomy*, New York: Academic Press.

Black, P.J. and Wiliam, D. (1998) *Inside the Black Box*, London: King's College London, School of Education.

Black, P.J., Harrison, C., Lee, C., Marshall, B. and Wiliam, D. (2002) *Working Inside the Black Box: Assessment for Learning in the Classroom*, London: King's College London, Department of Education and Professional Studies.

Black, P.J., Harrison, C., Lee, C., Marshall, B. and Wiliam, D. (2003) *Assessment for Learning: Putting it into Practice*, Buckingham: Open University Press.

Claxton, G. (2002) *Building Learning Power: Helping Young People Become Better Learners*, Bristol: TLO Limited.

Cotton, K. (1998) *Classroom Questioning* (School Improvement Research Series, Close-Up No. 5), Portland, OR: Northwest Regional Educational Laboratory.

De Bono, E. (1985) *Six Thinking Hats: An Essential Approach to Business Management*, Boston: Little, Brown & Company.

Department for Education (2014) *Teachers' Workload Diary Survey 2013 Research Report*, DFE-RR316. Available at www.gov.uk/government/publications.

Duckworth, A.L., Peterson, C., Matthews, M.D. and Kelly, D.R. (2007) 'Grit: perseverance and passion for long-term goals', *Journal of Personality and Social Psychology*, 92(6), 1087–1101.

Dweck, C.S. (2006) *Mindset: The New Psychology of Success*, New York: Random House Publishing.

Elder, Z. (2012) *Full on Learning: Involve Me and I'll Understand*, Carmarthen: Crown House Publishing.

Fisher, R. (2013) *Teaching Thinking: Philosophical Enquiry in the Classroom*, London: Bloomsbury.

Gilbert, I. (2007) *The Little Book of Thunks*, Carmarthen: Crown House Publishing.

Gilbert, I. (2010) *Why Do I Need a Teacher When I've Got Google?* Carmarthen: Crown House Publishing.

Hattie, J. (2009) *Visible Learning: A Synthesis of Over 800 Meta-Analyses Relating to Achievement*, Oxford: Routledge.

Higgins, S., Katsipataki, M., Kokotsaki, D., Coleman, R., Major, L.E. and Coe, R. (2014) *The Sutton Trust–Education Endowment Foundation Teaching and Learning Toolkit*, London: Education Endowment Foundation.

Hyerle, D. (2011) *Student Successes With Thinking Maps*, 2nd edition, Thousand Oaks, CA: Corwin.

Johnson, D.W. and Johnson, R.T. (2009) 'An educational psychology success story: social interdependence theory and cooperative learning', *Educational Researcher, 38*(5), 365–379. Available at www.co-operation.org/wp-content/uploads/2011/01/ER.CL-Success-Story-Pub-Version-09.pdf.

Kohn, A. (2011) 'The case against grades', *Educational Leadership Journal, 69*(3), 28–33.

Leahy, S., Lyon, C., Thompson, M. and Wiliam, D. (2005) 'Classroom assessment: minute by minute, day by day', *Educational Leadership, 63*(3), 19–24.

Martin, S. (2011) *Using SOLO as a Framework for Teaching*, Laughton, Sussex: Essential Resources Educational Publishing.

Marzano, R., Pickering, D. and Pollock J.E. (2001) *Classroom Instruction That Works*, Alexandria, VA: ASCD.

Maslow, A. (1943) 'A theory of human motivation', *Psychological Review, 50*(4), 370–396.

Meyer, B., Haywood, N., Sachdev, D. and Faraday, S. (2008) *Independent Learning: Literature Review, Learning and Skills Network*, London: Department for Children, Schools and Families, DCSF-RR051. Available at www.gov.uk/government/uploads/system/uploads/attachment_data/file/222277/DCSF-RR051.pdf.

Morgan, A. (2004) *The Pirate Inside*, New York: Wiley.

Prince, M. (2004) 'Does active learning work? A review of the research', *Journal of Engineering Education, 93*(3), 223–231. Available at http://www4.ncsu.edu/unity/lockers/users/f/felder/public/Papers/Prince_AL.pdf.

Thomas, D. and Brown J.S. (2011) *A New Culture of Learning: Cultivating the Imagination for a World of Constant Change*, Seattle, WA: Createspace.

Wilen, W.W. (1991) *Questioning Skills for Teachers*, 3rd edition, Washington, DC: National Education Association.

Wiliam, D. (2011) *Embedded Formative Assessment*, Bloomington, IN: Solution Tree Press.

Index

Accelerated Learning Contracts 152–3, 153*f*
accountability 115
active engagement 92; Auction House 97; Bowling 96; Catch the Bus 95; Freeze Frame 95–6; Memory Runs 92–3; Opinion Line 97–8; Post-it On 98; Revision Football 93–4; Splat 100; Trading Choices 99–100; The Writing's on the Window 94–5
Adobe Connect 137
AfL Dashboard 177–8
AfL Playing Cards 192–3, 192*f*
Always, Sometimes, Never 55
Answer Analyst 119
answers: Bad Answers 175–6; incorrect answers 32–3
Articulate 85–6
Ask the Teacher 135–6
assessment for learning 18–19, 173–4, 174*f*; baseline assessments 35, 36, 37*f*; effective feedback through marking 195–200; formative use of summative assessment 185–90; key principles 173–4; peer-assessment 190–5; progress not attainment 171; questioning to review progress 19, 179, 180–5; self-assessment 190, 202; sharing learning expectations 174–9; top ten marking time savers 200–2; *see also* data use in the classroom
assessment of learning *see* summative assessment
Auction House 97

Aurasma 138, 139
Automated Marking 201

Bad Answers 175–6
barriers to effective learning 64, 65*f*
Baseball Lessons 155–6
baseline assessments 35, 36, 37*f*
behaviour management *see* classroom management
the 'big picture' 15
Biggs, J. 155
Black, P.J. *et al.* 18–19, 173
Blackboard Collaborate 137
Blankety Blank 82–3
Bloom's Challenge Wall 147–9, 148*f*
Bloom's Taxonomy 29, 54, 147, 166
Board of Revision 75–6, 76*f*
Bonar, S. 83
Bowling 96
Buzan, T. 68

Catch the Bus 95
Centre for Learning and Performance Technologies 136, 142n4
challenge 63; *see also* differentiation
Challenge Corner 149–50
Challenge Envelope 150–1
Checkers 122
Checklists 175
choice 63, 109
Chunking 170
Clark, D. 57
classroom management 107–10, 110*f*; assume conformity 108; choice 63,

109; consistency 109; ignore secondary behaviour 109; instructional cues 108; meet and greet 108; partial agreement 109; pause and proximity 108; positive instruction 108; repair and rebuild 109

Claxton, G. 46

Cline, L. 22*f*, 23

Cluedo 86

collaborative learning 63, 112–15, 113*f*; fostering shared ownership of learning 116–21; group work 114, 115, 121–5; top ten digital tools 114, 136–41; *see also* collaborative learning structures

collaborative learning structures: Ask the Teacher 135–6; Creativity Carousel 133–4, 134*f*; Debates 132–3; Four-way Worksheets 131–2, 131*f*; Pass the Parcel Essay Writing 134, 135; Quiz Quiz Trade (QQT) 128–9; Silent Galleries 127–8; Speed Dating 129–31, 130*f*; Student Tutors 125–7, 126*f*; Think–Pair–Square–Share 128

Collaborize Classroom 140

Collis, K. 15

Colourful words 197–8

Comment Keys 202

community 115

competencies 64, 65*f*

Composite Answers 125

Comprehension Cranium 88–9, 89*f*

concept mapping tools 138

Conditions for Learning Model 64–6, 65*f*

confidence levels 36

conformity 108

Connect Four 59–60

Consider All Possibilities 47–8

consistency 109

contributing 138

Cotton, K. 28, 32

The Count 120–1

creative thinking 46; Consider All Possibilities 47–8; Creativity Wheel 48–50, 49*f*, 49*t*; Favourite Things 46–7

Creativity Carousel 133–4, 134*f*

Creativity Wheel 48–50, 49*f*, 49*t*

Cultural Reference Buddies 171

data use in the classroom 34; baseline sorting 35, 36, 37*f*; celebrate success 39, 40; confidence levels 36; effort rankings 40–1; The Exit Pass 36, 37; information-rich seating plans 37–8; progress flight paths 34, 35*f*, 36*f*; progress wall charts 39, 40*f*; spiky kids 38–9, 38*f*; trend spotting 41, 42*f*

De Bono, E. 178

Debates 132–3

decision maps 68, 70*f*

Diamond 9s 76, 77–8, 77*f*

Dictionary Dude 117

differentiation 17–18, 143–4, 144*f*; challenging through extension activities 18, 145–52; differentiation by choice 155–63; personalised learning 152–4; questioning to stretch and challenge 163–7; top ten strategies for support 167, 169–72

differentiation by choice 155; Going SOLO with Baseball 155–6; Independent Learning Projects (ILP) 157; Lessons that Flow 158–9, 158*f*; Taking the Credit 159–60, 160*t*; Targeted Objectives 160–1, 161*f*; Ten Minute Taste for Teaching 162–3; Thoughts and Crosses (Tic-tac-toe) 161, 162

digital tools for collaborative learning 114, 136, 139*f*; contributing 138; curating 137; flipping 136; hosting 137; inspiring 141; interacting 138, 139–40; managing 140; networking 137–8; quizzing 140; sharing 140–1

Disposition Doctor 120

dispositions 64, 65*f*

Dominoes 82

Dream Pictures 90–1

Dropbox 141, 147

Duckworth, A.L. *et al.* 61

Dweck, C.S. 61, 196

EAL Learners 39, 171–2

early bird activities 20

Edmodo 138
Educreations 136
effort rankings 40–1
Eisenhower, D.D. 14
Elder, Z. 17
engaging learners 73–5, 74*f*; active
    engagement 92–100; engaging with
    texts 87–91; game theory 75–87;
    making learning real 100–7; Rules of
    Engagement 74; top ten principles
    107–10, 110*f*
Engaging Learning Styles 169, 170
engaging with texts 87; Comprehension
    Cranium 88–9, 89*f*; Dream Pictures
    90–1; Ten-word Challenge 91; Text
    Trivia 89–90
English as an additional language (EAL)
    39, 171–2
Evernote 140
evidence-based research 3–5
Examining the Exam 188–9
The Exit Pass 36, 37
Exit Signs 51–2, 51*f*
Expert Groups 123–4
Explain Everything 136
exploded Venn diagrams 69, 70*f*
extension activities 18, 145; Bloom's
    Challenge Wall 147–9, 148*f*; Challenge
    Corner 149–50; Challenge Envelope 150–1;
    A Quick Response (QR) 145–7, 146*f*; Secret
    Mission 151; Thinking Extension 152

Facebook 137–8
Favourite Things 46–7
Feedback Grids 193, 194–5, 194*f*
Feedback Keys 200
feedback through marking 21, 63, 195;
    clarity 196; Colourful words 197–8;
    to grade, or not to grade? 195, 197,
    201; improvement 196; making
    improvement a priority 196, 199–200;
    marking frameworks 196*f*, 198; praise
    196; targets 196, 199; top ten marking
    time savers 200–2
Fisher, R. 44
Five Components of Outstanding
    Lessons/Learning 1–2, 2*f*, 4

Five for Five 189–90
Five Group Roles 121–3
Five-Part Lesson Plan 3, 14–21, 16*f*; 1:
    purpose 15, 17; 2: differentiation
    17–18; 3: formative assessment 18–19;
    4: lesson activities 20; 5: planning for
    progress 21; *see also* sample lesson
    plans
fixed mindsets 61
flipping the classroom 114, 136, 142n1
Focused Feedback 201
force-field analysis 68, 70*f*
formative assessment 18–19
formative use of summative assessment
    185; after the test 187–90; before the
    test 185–7
Four-way Worksheets 131–2, 131*f*
Freeze Frame 95–6

game theory 75; Blankety Blank 82–3;
    Board of Revision 75–6, 76*f*; Cluedo 86;
    Diamond 9s 76, 77–8, 77*f*; Dominoes
    82; Guess Who Quotes 87; Justification
    Jenga 85; Safe 78–9; Timed Talking
    85–6; Top Trumps 83–4, 84*f*; Wildcard
    Quizzes 79–81, 81*t*
Gatekeepers 122
Gervais, R. 73
getting stuck 18, 61, 62, 164–5, 165*f*
Gismos for teachers on the go 176–7
Glogster 139–40
Go Get Googler 118–19
Going SOLO with Baseball 155–6
grading work 195, 197, 201
graphic organisers for learning 68–72,
    70*f*; exploded Venn diagrams 69; force-
    field analysis 68; honeycomb 71; In and
    Out Box 71–2; mandala diagrams 69;
    matrix 71; mind maps 68; pie charts 72;
    spectrum 69; Three Buckets 71
grit 61
group work 114, 115; Composite Answers
    125; Expert Groups 123–4; Five Group
    Roles 121–3; Talking Tokens 124
growth mindsets 61–3
The Guardian 141
Guess Who Quotes 87

Half-finished Notes 169, 172
Happy Snappers 102–3
Hattie, J. 4
Hexagonal Learning 57–8
Hierarchy of Needs 113–14, 113*f*
Higgins, S. *et al.* 4–5
higher-order thinking 54; Always, Sometimes, Never 55; Connect Four 59–60; Hexlearning 57–8; Picture Wall 58–9, 59*f*; Question Box 54; Question Matrix 55–7
Hinge Questions 182–3, 183*f*
Hirst, K. 107
Home Peer Marking 200
homework: credit system 159–60, 160*t*; EAL learners 171; Home Peer Marking 200; modelling homework 175; Quick Turnaround Homework 171
honeycomb 70*f*, 71
Hudson, D. 32

improvement 196, 199–200
In and Out Box 70*f*, 71–2
In the News 101–2
independence 18
Independent Learning Projects (ILP) 157
Information Inquisition 120
inspiring 141
instructional cues 108
interactive resources 138, 139–40
interdependence 115
Interest Inventories 154

Jing 136
Jones, D. 106
Jones, J. 3
Jones, L. 26*f*, 27
Jukebox 104–5
Just Grade 201
Justification Jenga 85

Kagan, S. 128
Kelly, A. 175
The Khan Academy 141
Kipling, R. 55
Kohn, A. 195

leading teachers 3
learning expectations 174–5; AfL Dashboard 177–8; Bad Answers 175–6; Checklists 175; Gismos for teachers on the go 176–7; Thinking Hats Writing Frames 178–9, 179*f*
Learning Leaders 116, 118*f*; Answer Analyst 119; The Count 120–1; Dictionary Dude 117; Disposition Doctor 120; Go Get Googler 118–19; Information Inquisition 120; Objectives Overseer 117; Peer Praiser 121; Question Qualifier 119; Skills Selector 120; Time Technician 117; Wonder Worder 119
Learning Pyramid 125–6
learning reviews 19
learning styles 169, 170
lesson activities 20
lesson planning *see* data use in the classroom; Five-Part Lesson Plan; sample lesson plans
Lessons that Flow 158–9, 158*f*
Letters of Note 141
Live Modelling 170

McGovern, S. 24*f*, 25
Making a Statement 166, 167
mandala diagrams 69, 70*f*
Margin Marking 201
marking *see* feedback through marking; marking time savers
marking time savers 200; Automated Marking 201; Comment Keys 202; Feedback Keys 200; Focused Feedback 201; Home Peer Marking 200; Just Grade 201; Margin Marking 201; One to Mark 201; self-assessment and peer-assessment 202; Student Model Answers 200
Marzano, R. *et al.* 4
Maslow, A. 113, 113*f*
matrix 70*f*, 71
Medal and a Mission 198, 199*f*
meeting and greeting 108
Memory Runs 92–3
Mental Floss 141
metacognition 44, 45*f*

mind maps 68, 70*f*
mindsets 61–3
mini plenaries 19
Morgan, A. 71

National Training Labs 125
networking 137–8
new teachers 2–3
note-taking 169, 171
Now That's What I Call . . . 104–5

objectives and outcomes 15, 17
Objectives Overseer 117
One to Mark 201
Opinion Line 97–8

Padlet 138
partial agreement 109
Pass the Parcel Essay Writing 134, 135
pausing 108
Pearltrees 137
peer-assessment 190, 202; AfL Playing
    Cards 192–3, 192*f*; Feedback Grids 193,
    194–5, 194*f*; Home Peer Marking 200;
    Peer Marking 190–1; Peer Ordering
    191–2; RAG Reflections 193, 193*f*
Peer Praiser 121
personalised learning 152; Accelerated
    Learning Contracts 152–3, 153*f*; Interest
    Inventories 154
Picture Clues 169, 169*t*
Picture Wall 58–9, 59*f*
pie charts 70*f*, 72
Pinterest 137
Plant, N. 73
plenaries 20; mini plenaries 19; Socratic
    Plenary 52–4, 53*f*
Plenary Dice 50–1, 50*t*
Popplet 137, 138
positive instruction 108
Post-it On 98
PQA (Picture, Question, Answer) 184–5
praise 196
pre-starters 20
progress: EAL learners 171; flight paths
    34, 35*f*, 36*f*; planning for progress 21;
    questioning to review 19, 179, 180–5;
    wall charts 39, 40*f*

project management 140
proximity 108
Pupil Principal Examiners 186–7
purpose of lesson 15, 17

QR Codes 145–7, 146*f*
QRStuff 146, 147
Question Box 54
Question Matrix 55–7
Question Qualifier 119
questioning 28; incorrect answers 32–3;
    response techniques 31; techniques
    30–1; types of questions 28–9, 29*f*; wait
    time 32–3
questioning to review progress 19, 179;
    Hinge Questions 182–3, 183*f*; PQA
    (Picture, Question, Answer) 184–5;
    Questions under the Chair 183–4; The
    Review Wheel 180–2, 180*f*
questioning to stretch and challenge 163;
    Making a Statement 166, 167; Questions
    that FLOW 166, 167*f*, 168*t*; Solve It 164–
    6, 165*f*; A Token Question 163–4, 164*f*
Questions that FLOW 166, 167*f*, 168*t*
Questions under the Chair 183–4
A Quick Response (QR) 145–7, 146*f*
Quick Turnaround Homework 171
Quiz Quiz Trade (QQT) 128–9
Quizlet 140
quizzing 140

RAG Reflections 193, 193*f*
real-world connections 100; Happy
    Snappers 102–3; In the News 101–2;
    Now That's What I Call . . . 104–5;
    Special Guest 103–4; Tellin' Stories 106–
    7; Ten Minutes of TED 100–1; Voiceover
    105; X Factor Songs 105–6
Recorders 122
reflective thinking 50; Exit Signs 51–2,
    51*f*; Plenary Dice 50–1, 50*t*; Socratic
    Plenary 52–4, 53*f*
repair and rebuild 109
Reporters 122
researching topics 137
response techniques 31
The Review Wheel 180–2, 180*f*
Revision Football 93–4

Safe 78–9

sample lesson plans: 1: Religious Studies 22*f*, 23; 2: Spanish 24*f*, 25; 3: Design Technology 26*f*, 27

Scaffolding 170

Sceptics 122

Scoop.it 137

seating plans 37–8

Secret Mission 151

self-assessment 190, 202

self-esteem 19

setbacks 62

shared ownership of learning 116–21

sharing digital content 140–1

Sherrington, T. 35

Silent Galleries 127–8

Six Learning Junctions 61–3, 62*f*

Six Thinking Hats 178–9

skills for success 17, 64

Skills Icons 66–7, 67*f*

Skills Selector 120

SlideShare 141

social media 137–8

Socratic Plenary 52–4, 53*f*

Socrative 140

SOLO (Structure of Observed Learning Outcomes) Taxonomy 155

Solve It 164–6, 165*f*

special educational needs 18; *see also* EAL Learners

Special Guest 103–4

spectrum 69, 70*f*

Speed Dating 129–31, 130*f*

spiky kids 38–9, 38*f*

Splat 100

split-screen thinking 60–1; Conditions for Learning Model 64–6, 65*f*; Six Learning Junctions 61–3, 62*f*; Skills Icons 66–7, 67*f*; Thinking Word Cards 67, 68

starter activities 20, 53

statements 166, 167

strategies 5, 6, 7–13

Structure of Observed Learning Outcomes (SOLO) Taxonomy 155

Student Model Answers 200

Student Tutors 125–7, 126*f*

success 39, 40, 62, 65*f*

summative assessment 185; *see also* data use in the classroom; formative use of summative assessment

Summative Sound Bites 187–8

support *see* differentiation; support strategies

support strategies 167; Chunking 170; EAL Learners 39, 171–2; Engaging Learning Styles 169, 170; Half-finished Notes 169, 172; Live Modelling 170; Picture Clues 169, 169*t*; Quick Turnaround Homework 171; Scaffolding 170; Talking and Thinking Before Inking 170; Word Banks 167, 169, 169*t*

Taboo 85–6

Taking the Credit 159–60, 160*t*

Talking and Thinking Before Inking 170

Talking Tins 176–7, 177*f*

Talking Tokens 124

Targeted Objectives 160–1, 161*f*

targets 196, 199

teaching and learning geeks 3

Teaching and Learning Toolkit 4–5

teaching spectrum 114, 114*f*

TedEd 100, 141

The Telegraph 141

Tellin' Stories 106–7

Ten Minute Taste for Teaching 162–3

Ten Minutes of TED 100–1

Ten-word Challenge 91

Text Trivia 89–90

ThingLink 139–40

Think–Pair–Square–Share 128

Thinking Extension 152

Thinking Hats Writing Frames 178–9, 179*f*

thinking skills 44–6; creative thinking 46–50; higher-order thinking 54–60; metacognition 44, 45*f*; reflective thinking 50–4; split-screen thinking 60–8; top ten graphic organisers for learning 68–72, 70*f*

Thinking Word Cards 67, 68

Thoughts and Crosses (Tic-tac-toe) 161, 162

Three Buckets 70*f*, 71

Three to Go 185–7

thunks 141, 142n6

Time Technician 117
Timed Talking 85–6
Timekeepers 122
A Token Question 163–4, 164*f*
top tens: data use in the classroom 34–42;
 digital tools for collaborative learning
 114, 136–41; effective classroom
 management 107–10, 110*f*; graphic
 organisers for learning 68–72, 70*f*;
 marking time savers 200–2; quick
 reference quide 7–13; strategies to
 support students 167, 169–72
Top Trumps 83–4, 84*f*
Trading Choices 99–100
Trello 140
trend spotting 41, 42*f*
Twitter 137–8

Vimeo 140
virtual bulletin boards 137

virtual classrooms 137
visualisers 176, 177*f*
Voiceover 105
VoiceThread 138

webinar software 137
Wiederhold, C. 55
Wildcard Quizzes 79–81, 81*t*
Wilen, W.W. 28
Wiliam, D. 18–19, 185
Wonder Worder 119
Word Banks 39, 167, 169, 169*t*
World Changing 141
The Writing's on the Window 94–5

X Factor Songs 105–6

YouTube 140

Zwicky Box 48